I0420259

99 Bottles

by
ERIN LEE

Prologue

As a child, my family made monthly seven-hour trips to visit my grandparents in Eastern Pennsylvania. We filled the time, driving through sage New York countryside, singing songs. One favorite was "99 Bottles of Beer on the Wall." As we drove, I told my father about what my life would be like as an adult. With Mom and my four brothers sleeping, he listened to my plans:

I'd live in upstate New York—or close to it—and I'd marry a farmer. Our "forever house" would be lemon yellow; the color of my hair and the color of the dollhouse Dad made the summer I turned five. We'd live on a farm with at least one spotted cow. Her name would be Molly. I loved the smell of manure. I'd roll the windows down, close my eyes, and inhale as we passed New York dairy farms. Manure smelt of potential; of things growing.

We'd plant a huge garden each year and I'd pluck fresh green beans for dinner while Farmer— instead of Prince—Charming fed the cows. We'd have at least one son—the oldest—who'd be named after his daddy. The pair of them would be inseparable and the two great loves of my life. Maybe we'd have more children; at least two or three. I'd name my daughters Emily and Anastasia and we'd paint together in a meadow behind the farmhouse.

Our yard would host a tire swing from a maple tree for daydreaming. Blue jays and robins would settle in them, returning every year like family for the holidays. A willow tree, like the one at Greeley Park, would be my special place to hide and write. I'd pick fresh flowers every day. Daisies would brighten the wooden farmhouse breakfast table, where pulpy orange juice and kisses would be served every morning at nine, but not a minute sooner.

Dad would smile in the rear view mirror, waiting for me to finish, and tell me, "Sounds like you have a plan. But be careful what you wish for, hon." As I got older, he elaborated. He asked, "Do you know how much money farmers make?" or "Are you aware of how *liberal* people are in New York? New England is God's Country. You should stay put." I rolled my eyes, shrugged, and continued my singing; hoping to wake any one of my brothers so I'd have someone to play, or even fight, with. "...78 bottles of beer on the wall, 78 bottles of beer. You take one down, pass it around, 77 bottles of beer on the wall," I'd squawk. *Does he realize how liberal* Vermont *is? What's wrong with liberal, anyway?*

Seven hours is a long drive to a kid. You can do a lot of daydreaming, fantasizing, and planning in that time, especially when not one of your dumb brothers will even wake up for a pit stop at Arby's, a restaurant "God's Country" doesn't have. *Why didn't God give me a sister?* "...10 bottles of beer on the wall..."

We're far from alone.

Consider these statistics from the National Association for Children of Alcoholics:

    * Seventy six million Americans, about 43 percent of the U.S. adult population, have been exposed to alcoholism in the family.

    * Roughly one in eight American adult drinkers is an alcoholic or experiences problems due to the use of alcohol. The cost to society is estimated at in excess of $166 billion each year.

    * Separated and divorced men and women are three times as likely as married men and women to say they had been married to an alcoholic or problem drinker.

    * Almost two-thirds of separated and divorced women, and almost half of separated or divorced men, under age 46, have been exposed to alcoholism in the family at some time.

Dedication

For the spouses and children of alcoholics. You are not alone. I pray you find the answers you seek.

For those who struggle with substance abuse and knowing how to ask the questions you need answers to.

99 Bottles   **ERIN LEE**

Also for

My children, whom I've relied on a little too much but promise never to serve meatloaf to. Thanks for being the most important chapters in my life. You were my beginning and my love for you will never change its mind.

People who make dark corner wedding day bets: Sorry, not sorry. Next time, bet on love or don't bet at all just because it's the nice thing to do. It's better to lose five bucks than to hurt people. The world is hard enough.

Everyone who will insist this is a straight *memoir and jump to judgement: Try again. For those who think I'm writing about them,* maybe *and* probably *I am. Thank you for being a part of* my *journey, for better or worse.*

Clients who've told me I don't "get it" because I've never known an alcoholic; who said I could not possibly understand their choices. For the woman who told me my life was "perfectly together" and it'd be impossible for me to know without having been there. I admire your courage to share your story with me anyway.

Lastly, for my soulmate: My heart. I'll bet on you, for you, and with you—any day, any place, any time. Our story is to be continued until "The End".

Table of Contents

Author's Note

"This novel has been a labor of love.
It is the most challenging book I will ever write
and will be the hardest to release into a critical
world. It is also so much more:
It is a love story and letter; a plea for forgiveness
and an offer of it too.
I wrote it to help people who struggle with code-
pendency; something I felt was important to do.
Those are my reasons and they are enough."

-ERIN LEE

* * *

I've divided chapters of this book into sections
based on the song Lisa sang as a child. For those
who aren't familiar, "99 Bottles of Beer on the
Wall" works its way down through the bottles until
there are no more bottles of beer.

This book is not a memoir. Parts of it started out
that way, and, like things do, it evolved. I felt it
was more important to tell a shared story rather
than just my own. Over the seven years I've picked
at this, it has become a work of fiction based on
the lives of many people struggling with substance
abuse. It is a product of many perspectives of those
whom I encounter daily in my work as a therapist,
as well as personal experiences.

I have used humor in places in this book not because I believe the topic is anything to laugh about.

Instead, it's because I believe that the ability to laugh at oneself or situation is a big part of what gets us through the tough times. In laughter, we find healing, forgiveness, and peace. In no way do I mean to trivialize the topic of alcoholism or any other form of addiction. Instead, I write to understand the fragile waltz between addicts, enablers, and co-dependents. I *need* to understand it because I am one of them.

It is my hope that through Lisa's story, readers will come to appreciate more about their own dances with loved ones who struggle with addiction and/or the impact addiction has on the ones you love. I know that I have. It's only in asking the questions that—together—we will find answers to bring us peace.

***

THIS NOVEL DEALS WITH THE TOPIC OF ALCOHOLISM AND UNDIAGNOSED MENTAL HEALTH ISSUES AND COULD BE DISTURBING TO SOME READERS. READER DISCRETION IS ADVISED.

***

THIS BOOK IS NOT A MEMIOR.
IT IS A WORK OF FICTION BASED ON THE EXPERIENCES OF THIS WRITER AND MANY CLIENTS WHOM SHE'S WORKED WITH WHO STRUGGLE WITH LOVING AN ADDICT.

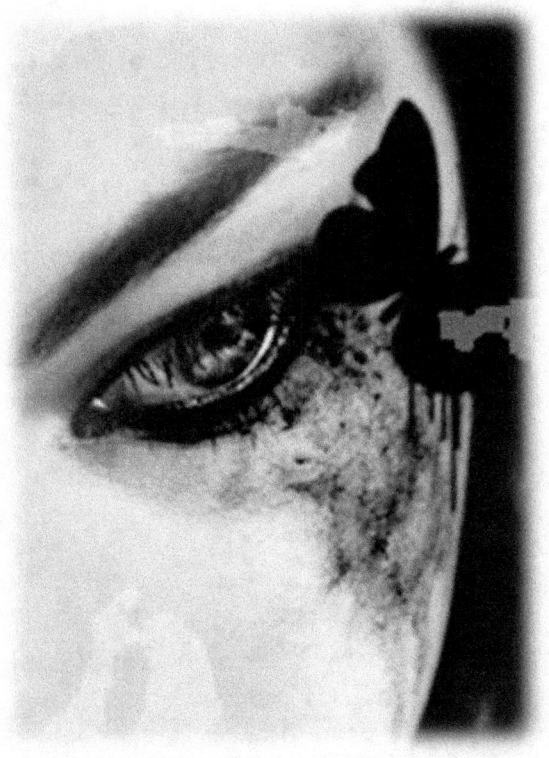

Introduction

"My name is Lisa. I'm forty-two years old and the mother of three. I'm an enabler. I'm sad. I'm hopeful. I'm scared. Like so many others, I don't know what to do. This is *my* story. Yet somehow, I believe it's also *our* story."

99 Bottles: Farmer Charming
"I'm not brave enough for this."

2010

I can't take my eyes off of their love-making.
He sips at her, letting her rest on his lips before
swallowing; allowing her to consume him until
they switch. I watch them—my husband and his
mistress of a dozen years or more—and their
dance. I cannot hate her; the other woman. I've
practically invited her in. I've allowed her to exist;
turned a blind eye, paid for her services, and even
participated in threesomes: My husband, his mistress, and I.

They see each other regularly—three to four
hours at a time, every other night—until he finally
collapses beneath her. He sleeps, alone, in our marriage bed with dreams orchestrated by what she's
done to him, for him, with him. What she will do
again, next time.

I can taste her on his breath when he kisses me
goodnight. When he's gone, I rub her on my sleeve
and wrinkle my nose. She's in our sheets and cur-
tains too. It's been this way almost as long as I remember—my husband and his mistress, together
since the late nineties, before I quite caught on.
Back when I thought it was innocent flirtation.

Should it really surprise me, or anyone, that I'd
want revenge? Somehow, it does. I ignore my guilt
as I leap from the couch and pour what's left of her

down the sink. *That will show him. Good riddance to them both: Him and Ms. Labatt's. She is, after all, his favorite type of beer.*

***

Daily thought of an enabler: *But (insert name)'s a* good *drunk.*

It's true. There *are* different types of alcoholics. I would know. I've been to enough meetings. Better, I'm married to one. It's just that it isn't so black and white. As with most things, drunks come in all shades of gray.

I used to tell myself my husband was a "good drunk". Now, I'm not so sure. I'll get back to that later. What I *have* learned is that no two alcoholics are identical. None are all good and none are all bad. What they *do* have in common is that they all get the same reputation; they are broken and sometimes dangerous. We hear about them beating their kids, being in car accidents, and being unreliable and sloppy. The truth is, not every drunk drinks from the moment they wake up until the moment they fall asleep.

There are those who make time for sobriety and hold, often stressful, jobs. They take momentary interest in the people who love them. Some put their drinking schedules aside—even if only for a few hours—to attend family events or put on an abstemious face for curious neighbors. They live behind ivy-laced fences and put extra money in church collection baskets. They are the types professionals call "functional alcoholics". We all know them, even if we don't know it yet. We probably even like or depend on them.

Likewise, not all alcoholics are angry or violent. Instead, there are the "happy drunks". Some of the nicest, most outwardly happy people I've ever known couldn't stay sober for a straight week if their lives depended on it. Yet, they go out of their way to make other people smile and are the first to offer a hand or open a door—even if stumbling.

"Pragmatic drunks" are like pharmacists. They rationalize their drinking as an acceptable way to medicate pain. They see their nightly cocktail regimens as antidepressants—a cheaper version of the pills so many of us pop without thought because a doctor gave us permission. These self-medics have too much pride to see a psychiatrist or ask for help. They view themselves as honorable because they have found a way to handle their pain, they think, without hurting anyone.

There are the soccer parents who sip rum and coke from water bottles on the sidelines. They come armed with breath spray and Mentos to cover their chic solution to worry. It not unlike yoga or a trip to the tanning booth, they reason. They can be found in PTA meetings and volunteering to make cupcakes for one too many birthdays. They have never said no to a car pool. They are the "invisible alcoholics". That is, until they kill someone. Or themselves. Or someone else's kid. And then everyone is surprised. No one saw it coming. Everyone wonders why.

I could list other types for days, but you get the point. If I *had* to pick, my husband is—for the

14

most part—a "good drunk". At least, that's what he tells himself. It's what I tell myself on nights like this too. Lately, it's been working less and less. He's sleeping now; better known as passed out. Silly sober me can't sleep. Ironically, I'm the one who is invisible, but I'm not an alcoholic. I've just finished making cupcakes for my daughter's recital reception and can't say no either. I want to say no. I want to say a lot of things, but I keep my mouth shut and settle in for another night of status quo. I'm a "good wife".

***

Dozens of flies flirt at the tired mouths of nine empty beer cans on the kitchen counter. *Where are they coming from? Is it the cow? Maybe they just came in to join the party?* I swat at them. The house is quiet. I don't allow myself to collect the cans for the recycling bin. Instead, I watch wings slap against the cold blue metal that has helped shape the last decade of my life. The children sleep peacefully in our finished basement, oblivious to another night of their father's drinking. My sons dream of soccer and baseball games and cute girls with names like Kenzie, Morgan, and Taylor. My daughter wishes on dandelions for a new art set and prays that the kids at school will stop teasing her for being the teacher's pet.

I wonder, sometimes, if she dreams in color. Several rooms away, from my perch on the couch, I can hear the steady drum of his snores. It's nearly midnight. He's been out cold since nine. *Maybe nine is his lucky number.* I laugh, cracking the silence the way he cracks beer cans. *Stop. This isn't funny. This is your life. Do something.*

I stare up at the butterflies I painted six years ago on the dining room ceiling. Undisciplined, they seem to be winking at me now—asking what my next move is. In no mood to be tested, I look away. My eyes return to the drunken flies in our kitchen. They skitter in beer puddles, back and forth to the Jacuzzi formerly known as the sink. *At least someone else had fun at his little party. Can flies wake up with hangovers?*

***

There is no denying my love for Jeff. Or maybe it's my own emptiness that keeps me here. Perhaps it's my need to be drunk on his love that propels me to the kitchen to clean up his messes. I place my teacup in the sink for the night, shooing away the uninvited party guests, and turn out the lights. As I open the bedroom door, my nose curls to the strong scent of Labatt's Blue mixed with his sweat. I decide to breathe through my mouth but the scent is so overwhelming I can taste it. Sensing me, he pulls back the blankets and brings me into him tight—like the passionate lover he once was. I hold my breath, close my eyes, and drift off, remembering a time when there were no flies.

A butterfly skitters across our pasture. Her movements are effortless. Her wings carry her high above the dandelions and sun-stroked daisies. She's drunk, not on nectar, but on life. Her destina-

tion is unknown and she's neither flying toward, nor away from anything. I reach for her; willing my own transformation.

***

1996

I check my teeth three times in the rearview mirror before taking a deep breath and stepping out of my white 1987 Nissan 200SX. I smile to myself, running my tongue over bride-white teeth as I press my lips together. *Check! Thank God for braces...and good lipstick.* Winter stings my chipmunk cheeks as I wrap a black scarf tighter around my jean jacket. I glance back in a side mirror to see how my ass looks. *Good. Not bad. Good. The new jeans were worth it.*

I don't bother locking my door as I head for the airport. No one in Vermont locks their doors, even at the airport. I am certainly not worried about anyone stealing my nine-year-old, $2,500 lemon, whom I like to call Bertha. Every car I'd ever owned—now a total of two—is named Bertha.

I check my pink plastic watch, the one I bought from Ames department store only a week before. It's 7:42 p.m. *Shit. I told him seven. Forty-two minutes late. I hope he's still here.* I jog to the United Air terminal. We'd agreed to meet at the airport because it's public. I wanted to be safe, having never spent time together in person before. He'd been amenable to this. "I want you to feel safe. That's important to me," he'd said.

99 Bottles

As I open the heavy terminal doors at Burlington Airport, I see him. I look away, but not before taking a full inventory of him. He is smaller than I'd pictured. I generally prefer a guy with broader shoulders and a bit of a pot belly. Stocky guys make oversized-me feel tinier and more feminine. But his chestnut hair, complete with 90210 sideburns, and the way he wears his faded tan cowboy boots make my heart thump—hard. I watch him with my peripheral vision as I march past him like a solider to the escalators in front of me. I can feel his mocha eyes tracking me. I know he's wondering if I am the girl he has been waiting for. *Let him wonder. I'm not brave enough for this.*

I need time. And by now, I am about fifty minutes short on that. I hadn't been nervous only hours before, picking out the new Levi's at TJ Maxx. Instead, I'd been giddy and focused on the task at hand. My plan was simple: *Make the cute boy from Rhode Island drool.* Now, seeing him, things are different. My palms are moist and shake in my black gloves as my legs pull me toward the ATM machine. *Make it look like you're getting money.*

Money? Am I even going to need *money? I spent everything on this outfit. Dumb. Dumb. Dumb.*

He doesn't know, for sure, it's you. He doesn't know it's you. It's not too late to get out of here.

No. You can't *do that. It's* mean. *He drove all this way. Rhode Island to Vermont: That's no joke. That's a trip. And those boots. You might just be okay. Stay calm.*

I fiddle with the ATM machine, drain my account of its last $40, and talk myself into a quick trip to the ladies room for a last-minute pep talk. It's after eight now and he is checking his watch when I finally approach him on an airport bench. I stand above him, noting the smell of Cool Water cologne—one of my favorites—as he looks up at me. His smile is thin, but warm.

"Lisa?"

"Jeff? Hi. Yes. It's me. How are you?" *Awkward.*

Our full two weeks of nightly three-hour phone calls hasn't been enough to settle his nerves. His hands shake worse than mine had only moments before. I fiddle with my scarf, debate for a moment, and reach to hug him. He returns my hug with a loud exhale and a firm hold. *Not bad for a skinny guy.*

"Are you okay? You look a little nervous," I say, figuring it's best to get it out in the open.

"I was thinking you weren't coming." He frowns. A deep wrinkle settles in his forehead, mimicking the frown on his thin lips.

"Oh, gosh. I'm so sorry! I didn't mean to make you worry about that. I'd never have stood you up. I just got, well, busy," I assure him. "I mean, I guess the *truth* is I'm never really on time. Sorry." I look down at the floor, memorizing the pattern in the linoleum tiles.

"It's okay. I'm just glad you're here."

I sprout up. "So, what do you think? Do I look like my picture?"

Part of me wants to pinch myself to be sure it is really me talking. Here I am, talking to a gorgeous potential Farmer—not prince, I don't want a prince—Charming in cowboy boots. A Farmer Charming I've already shared my deepest secrets with during all-nighters on the phone and I'm not nearly as nervous as I should be. Instead, I rub his back as we walk out of the terminal, hoping to keep him from feeling as nervous as he looks.

"Yes. You're pretty," he finally says, staring at his boots while we walk. My eyes follow his, noticing how clean they are. *Maybe he went shopping too.* I wonder how he knows I am pretty. *I could have one eye and be missing a nose for all he knows. He's barely looked at me.*

"Where do you want to go? I know of a great place to go dancing! Or are you hungry? Would you rather go get something to eat?" *Stop. You're being manic.*

"I can't eat right now. Nerves. But if you're hungry?"

I swallow my disappointment. *No need to tell him I use food as valium.*

"I'm good. Let's go dance and we can get something to eat later. How's that?"

He smiles, opening the door for me. "Sounds good! "

"So, are you a good dancer?" I ask.

He smiles without hesitation. It's so wide I think his lips will crack.

"Yeah. I can dance."

I gulp, cursing my two left feet. *Shit. I'm dead. Guys aren't supposed to know how to dance. Only*

I would find the only cowboy in all of New England who can dance.

***

Present day

My shrink told me to pay attention to the things I do, not the things I say or think. She said, when looking at my life, to try to diagnose myself in every situation. She told me I need to get in the habit of doing this to help me understand my choices and behaviors. She said we can't change history if we don't recognize when we're repeating it. Honestly, I'm not one for shrinks, but I figured it was worth a shot, and lord knows I've had enough therapy to be able to do this. Self-Diagnosis there, in 1996: Young, naive, insecure, innocent, and hopeful. It wasn't a pathology, yet. But just wait. These are the things enablers are made of.

***

Self-diagnosis: Believer in happy endings.

98 Bottles: Turbos & Diapers
"How was I to know?"

He wasn't always *a drinker.* That's what I tell myself almost daily. It's my way of forgiving myself for choosing a man who could throw away so much of his life on alcohol. People who love drinkers become pathological liars. It's part of the job. But there was, indeed, a time before his skin was as pale as wax and his eyes went dead: A time *before* we joked about whether or not he'd die of cirrhosis.

Jeff and I met in our early twenties. I used our ages to justify our bi-weekly binge trips to the bar. *Everyone our age drinks,* I assured myself. The bar, Turbo's, in Providence, Rhode Island, just happened to be directly across the street from the duplex we were renting. It was our first home together and its proximity to the local bar made for easy excuses to go out for cocktails to burn off steam.

Money was always an issue for us, but it was particularly bad back then. Jeff was a full time college student. I, a recent college graduate, was looking for work as a journalist while waiting tables at a restaurant that catered to seniors and offered $6.99 grilled halibut lunchtime specials. Our combined income was less than $20,000 a year. On Friday nights, when my tip apron was at its heaviest, we'd take the dollar bills to Turbo's for last call and splurge on our favorites. It was draft beer for him and White Russians for me.

Young, in love, and engaged to be married the following year, we didn't see anything wrong with our Friday night ritual. This was hardly the six-day-a-week partying I'd done in college as a Kappa pledge. Twenty-one, finally legal, and with the man I'd dreamt of, our first months together were some of our happiest.

Foggy Friday nights often lead to drunken sex. Combine young lust with heavy doses of antibiotics for bronchitis and you have a recipe for, well, a miracle. *Surprise, surprise!* Ill-timed or not, I couldn't have been happier when, in August of 1996, I learned I was six weeks pregnant. Our weekly trips to Turbo's halted and nine months, one shot gun wedding later, we were the proud parents of a little boy—also named Jeff, (JJ) after his daddy. Everything was going exactly to plan, even if it was a bit rushed. As far as I was concerned, all we needed was a hobby pitchfork and a lemon farmhouse. Well, that and a little money to buy a cow.

Two years, and minimal alcohol later, we had another son, Nathan. Jeff was back in school, trying to further his career in the health field, and I was working full time as a reporter. By night, Jeff worked third shift at a warehouse to help pay the bills and I stayed up with Nathan. Issues with our landlords—who insisted that it was perfectly normal to blast rock music at 2 a.m. on a Tuesday morning—prompted us to move northwest to upstate New York as Jeff entered his last semester in Vermont. His commute was grueling. I landed a job as a full time reporter at a daily paper and he split his time between classes and working as a carpenter; his first career. The long commute to his classes, coupled with money problems that came from increased rent, pulled Jeff to the bottle. I was left juggling the boys and a full time job. I hardly had time to count his empty bottles, nor was I brave enough to try.

Jeff's drinking began with one six-pack every Friday night. At first, I didn't think much of it. *After all, he really is stressed out,* I reasoned. When you love an alcoholic, you also become a master at justifying things. Working, going to school full time, and sharing the responsibilities of two children under age three was definitely a lot to juggle for any young couple. We were still in love, but beginning to understand what our parents meant when they'd told us not to be in such a rush to grow up. It was 2001, the 9/11 attacks were fresh and we were two kids trying to figure out how to make our own way.

I turned to my tattered journal—named Mr. Journal or Mr. J for short—often during this time. As Jeff's drinking increased, so did the frequency of my midnight scribblings with Mr. J:

November 5, 2001
Dear Mr. Journal,
He's drinking every other night lately. I can't take this. I feel like I don't have a husband every other night of the week. I want to tell someone so

badly. I feel like I am living alone. I don't know who to talk to. I want to help him so bad.

If I tell someone, I'm betraying him. I don't understand why he does this. It's so hard watching him do this. I hate that I can hear him breathing right now. It is only a reminder that he is so close by, but I can't go to bed with him. The smell of the booze makes me cringe. I hate alcohol. I hate everything about it. Maybe if I did something better—was a better wife—he would stop drinking.

November 23, 2001

Nathan came running up to me today with an empty beer can. He'd been sipping at it, smiling, and telling me he was "like Daddy". The kid isn't even two yet! I felt horrible when I took it away from him and told him "no!" He looked at me like I was an evil monster.

Why doesn't Jeff see that Nate worships him? Why doesn't he realize that the kids are watching every move he makes? He's such a good person. He's honest and he's caring. He's loving. Why does he let beer change him?

I look in his eyes and there is so much sadness. I don't know how to help him. I want to help him with everything inside of me. But nothing works. I ask him how I can help and he responds, "with a dirt nap," or, "Let me hang myself in the backyard."

I don't know what I'm going to do. I know he's depressed. He won't admit it. He won't do anything about it. I feel so helpless.

I asked him not to drink around the kids. He gave me a dirty look. Maybe I'll ask him again when he's sober.

November 28, 2001

He told me long before we got married about his issues with depression. He'd had it on and off as a kid, he'd said. I didn't think much of it. I didn't understand depression back then. I'd never had it. I mean, I was a happy kid: Wasn't I?

I never knew how serious depression could be. The first time Jeff was depressed around me, I was so naive that I offered him orange juice—thinking orange juice cures anything. How stupid could I have been?

Now I'm wondering if he's bipolar or something. I've talked to him about getting on antidepressants but he will hear no such thing. He doesn't want to go to a therapist to talk about his problems. Apparently he has not had good experiences with counselors and says it's "not manly".

I want to scream. I want to scream, "It's not manly to be drunk by seven every night either!" Instead, as usual, I smile, rub his head, and tell him everything is going to be okay.

Then? When everyone is asleep? I cry myself to sleep.

January 23, 2002

I don't even know where to begin tonight. It disgusts me. Whatever happened to a six-pack on a Friday night only? He's already had eleven beers so far and is showing no sign of slowing down. I actually miss the stupid six-packs! I need to talk to someone. This is going from bad to worse too fast. I don't want to embarrass him. I don't want to embarrass myself. Everyone said we didn't know each other long enough before we got married. They don't know how well we get along when he's sober. Did I miss something with the drinking thing? I mean, when we met, I drank too. I didn't see this coming. Duh. Why didn't he stop when we had the boys? I stopped. It wasn't even difficult!

Some writer somewhere once said that whatever struggles you go through are actually blessings: They are raw material for your writing. If that's the case, I should have a lot of material when I tell him I'm pregnant. Again. Maybe this time it will be a girl. Maybe that will change his mind, help him, something. Maybe he will do it for her. He wouldn't want <u>his</u> daughter married to an alcoholic, would he?

***

Drinking issues aside, it didn't take long for me to learn more about who my husband really was. Having only dated for a year before marrying, I'd been so enamored by my fantasy version of him that it took a while to defog my love-blind eyes and fully see him for who he really was. But it was a process; a slow unravelling of tiny details.

I quickly learned, as much as he despised it, that my Farmer Charming was also a Rhode Island guy, through and through; two things that didn't match. Raised from the age of thirteen in the wealthiest part of the tiny state, Jeff had all the tastes and markings of the thoroughbreds he grew up with. This was quite different from the simple, blue collar farmer I thought I'd signed up for. While he'd prefer to tell it that he was forced to adapt to the ways of his affluent peers, he came to me with a personal affinity for brand names and all things quality; reminiscent of his private Catholic school education. "Quality is so much better than quantity, hon," he'd plea to me every spring when I asked him what he wanted for his birthday. "I know you'd rather have a hundred candles from the dollar store than one Tiffany lamp, but I'm not that way." I'd shrug, and try to choose something of a compromise like, say, fifty gas lanterns. He'd smirk when he opened the gifts, sure he had many years ahead in training me. Eventually, I got it, and now I head straight to the expensive brand name outlets for his birthday.

My husband came to me knowing how to tie a tie, preferably a hundred percent silk tie, with his eyes shut. Or, more often, in the dark while I blissfully snored in our California king bed. To this day, Jeff owns a total of three $75 Ralph Lauren polo shirts. One of them is missing. His tee shirts, all Adidas, come in three colors; navy, gray, and royal blue. In 2003 I gave up trying to convince him that he could have a dozen "regular" polo shirts from Walmart and that the five for $20 tees at Olympic sports were more practical than the $48 ones he preferred.

In many ways, Jeff's personality is as predictable as his wardrobe. When he has something difficult to tell me, he paces the house and scratches his back on the corner wall in our kitchen. He rises every morning at 5:30 to take care of the animals and is in bed by no later than nine, even on weekends. He spends all of his free time working in the yard. A generous piece of land, he single-handedly managed to clear about two acres of our lot to make room for a barn for our cows. He does this, of course, in his $100 Adidas indoor soccer sneakers, sometimes with a beer in his hand. I've learned not to cringe.

It never fails to surprise me how deep this man actually is. Sometimes, I believe it's the depth to him—bottomless—that's allowed me to believe in him and stick with our marriage during our rockiest times. Jeff has this effect on everyone who knows him well. Now a director for a multimillion dollar homecare nursing agency, he's had countless employees tell him he is the best boss they have ever had. One woman, a frazzled and feisty sixty-four-year-old he was forced to fire, told him he was the smartest person she'd ever met. I view her now as another example of how he's someone people want to hate, but never can. It's just his way. That woman still sends us Christmas cards.

True to any farmer's nature, Jeff is an avid animal lover. He speaks to animals with a chew-toy voice, greeting them with nicknames and giving them kisses. The first time I visited his mother's house I was greeted by three oversized boxers and an English mastiff. Having grown up with no animals in my family home, these three canines scared the hell out of me. Their fur and jumpy nature quickly turned my asthmatic self into a world-class-wheezer. *Get me out of here! God, they smell.* But Farmer Charming was patient, helping me to understand what he saw in animals; even ones who shit on the floor every morning and go by the names of Boomer and Bingo.

While he claims to be a jack of all trades, master of none, Farmer Charming is the man everyone calls when they need help with anything. When you need a corporate staffing or marketing issue handled, call Jeff. Kitchen sink clogged? 1-800-Call-Jeff. Need a hug? Yep, you guessed it.

Jeff is the type of guy who stops on roadsides for women and children with car troubles, holds the door open behind him, listens patiently to employees' personal issues, and puts loose change—sometimes twenty dollar bills that we really can't afford to spare—into the drive thru bucket at McDonald's for kids with cancer. He's also the type who allows his writer wife to record and document every up and down of their marital life without wincing or throwing around ultimatums. "Write from your heart. Who gives a fuck what people think?" he says. "No one can judge me but God. I don't care what you write about me. As long as you're happy, hon." He doesn't just say it. He means it. Jeff doesn't believe in keeping secrets; for any reason. I've always envied that self-assuredness. I just wish he could fully understand what would truly make me happy: Writing a book about our sober life.

Stern in his parenting style, Farmer Charming is the first person to threaten to charge the kids for a portion of the hefty electric bill when they leave the lights on overnight. He's also the first to forget about it when the electric bill comes and regularly declines their feeble offers of report card money reparations. Farmer Charming is the kind of guy who would take his daughter bra shopping while secretly wanting to die.

***

2002

We're driving to Springfield, Mass for a respite weekend. His mother is going to watch the kids for us while we spend a few days together home alone. We are both anxious to drop the boys off. We've grown excited about the idea of adding another child—surprise or not—to our brood. We hope for a girl—certain the third time will be the charm. Nathan is cutting teeth and JJ is an active four year old with a pension for banging full-fisted on his bedroom door for hours when he doesn't get his way. About five minutes before arriving at our agreed upon meeting place, we drive past a man holding a sign reading "Will Work for Food. Any Bit Helps." The man wears a tan cargo jacket, about three sizes too small. Its seams are yelling "please help us" almost as loud as his sign. I know Jeff's intention before he makes a U-Turn and pulls into a Wendy's restaurant. He orders four junior cheeseburgers and promptly delivers them to the man. The man's face lights up as my husband reaches out the broken window of our mud brown Dodge and hands him his last dollars' worth of hamburgers. "God bless you, man," Jeff says, smiling.

It's countless experiences like this that made me realize early on what a gem I had in my husband. I was protective of him from the get-go. These qualities are what I'd remind myself of when I wrote journal entries that screamed, "What the hell are you doing with this alcoholic prick?" These qualities helped me live in denial and to rationalize.

***

In most ways, our opposite personalities compliment us. The saying goes that opposites attract and likes stick together. But in our case, after two decades together, Jeff and I have learned the art of compromise and play well on each other's strengths and weaknesses. Jeff is the sort of person for whom every transaction boils down to basic math. The amount of money a man makes defines him as a provider. The number of times he says, "I love you," shapes him as a husband. The amount of hours he spends playing with the kids is what makes him a good father. I've always been horrible at math, have never cared about material things or bottom line income, and regularly lose track of time in a book while waiting for my kids to finish practices.

Jeff is practical in situations others would find sentimental. When Nathan was born, he made sure to pack extra socks and double-checked with doctors that it would be okay for his big brother to visit "with all those germs little kids can bring in." I, on the other hand, pulled JJ onto my stomach and encouraged him to curl up with his new brother merely an hour after he was born. *Germs be dammed. A little dirt makes for a healthy soul.* Of course, my feet were warm when the three of us napped together in the hospital bed, thanks to my plan-ahead husband.

When we walk together, Jeff holds my hand for safety, not romance. And yet, something about this is very romantic to me. He, who walks with the assurance of a proud lion and finesse of a cheetah, often checks to be sure I'm in no danger of tripping over carpet lint. Sometimes, I wonder if I actually would fall without his hand to hold. This may be part of what's kept me here all these years.

***

Self-Diagnosis: Co-dependent.

97 Bottles: The Neighbors
"What happens in the neighborhood
stays in the neighborhood."

The oldest and only daughter in a family of five children, my parents still had the energy to keep a close eye on me growing up. Curfews, monitored phone calls, and Mom's occasional whiff test for the slightest hint of smoke on my breath were bookends to my childhood. Later, the opposite would be true when my youngest brother Joshua— Josh—made his debut into the world. More than twenty years of raising children, realizing "this too shall pass," and making their fair share of live-and-learn mistakes had my parents in a coma by the time Joshua hit his late teens. A decade and a half younger than me, Josh flaunted his blatant disregard for flimsy—more like "just a suggestion"— parental rules right around the time Jeff's drinking became a major problem. From time to time, Joshua called me, telling me stories of drug experimentation and, "Screw it, dude, you just gotta live your own life." I took those calls as I was carrying my own husband to bed. No one had any clue.

I reminded Josh of the dangers of drugs and alcohol, stressing that they can ruin lives. He laughed, telling me our parents didn't even care, so "why should I?" Often, I struggled with which of Josh's secrets to keep and which to share with my parents. Hinting at problems "bigger than you realize," I finally decided to stay out of it after Mom reminded me "there are some things a parent doesn't want to know." *Is she kidding me? The kid is going to end up in jail and she wants to pretend like it's not happening?* But I also felt that, in ratting him out, I'd be cutting off a safe support system for him. I knew, too well, how important that sort of thing could be. I desperately wished I had a big sister of my own to confide in. I felt sad that Ella wouldn't have one either.

Jeff met Josh when he was seven. When my folks sat Jeff down at the kitchen table in 1995 to grill him on his career plans, it was Josh who helped Jeff—one to avoid social situations at all costs—escape. "Dude! Come play with me," Josh would beg. Then, they'd march off to a game of Nintendo.

"He's so good with Joshy," Mom said.

"Thank God for Josh," Jeff said.

I said nothing. *There are some things a parent doesn't want to know.*

I hid Jeff's secret from our families from the very start. In fact, it took me more than half a decade to reveal it to anyone at all. Keeping secrets was nothing new for me. Raised nearly single handedly—Dad was around but worked a lot and had very little understanding of the way a girl's mind worked—by a very strict mother who often blamed her excessive screaming fits on premenstrual stress, I learned early on to do everything I could to appear perfect. I failed miserably, but lied to myself about it anyway.

I grew up hating conflict and yelling. I wanted everyone to think I had it all together. An alcoholic

35

husband would only publicly prove I had failed. On top of that, I felt a strong sense of loyalty to a man who I knew sincerely loved me for me. Telling other people about his problem seemed like the highest form of betrayal. Of course, there was also that ever-present fear of being judged: *What will the neighbors think?* No matter how hard I'd tried to avoid it, my mother's fears were in me like our shared blood type. The funny part? I don't even know my neighbors now. And I certainly don't care what they think. I make a habit of *trying* to stay out of other people's business—*trying.*

"The neighbors" were everything when I was a kid. My childhood neighborhood resembled a dysfunctional family. The rules were simple: Everyone knew everyone. Everyone pretended to like everyone. And everyone talked about everyone behind everyone's backs. Your best bet in that neighborhood? Don't give them anything to talk about. *What is that saying? Keep your friends close, keep your enemies closer?* That was Pine Street. Anyone who lived there longer than a few years— which was pretty much everyone except those "hoodlums" at the end of the street with the wild, overgrown lawn—knew it.

In fifth grade I was friends with a plump, but popular girl named Donna. Donna and I twirled batons and played with our Cabbage Patch Kids for hours after school each day. We shared secrets and our first crush on the same boy. Donna, the youngest in her family, was much cooler than I was. She had a big sister who made sure she dressed in the right clothes, she knew older kids, and she wasn't afraid to make new friends. I, on the other hand, was awkward. Taller than any of the boys in our grade and shier than I'd ever let on to my outspoken mother, I did my best to remain invisible. I secretly felt Donna was doing me a favor by being my friend. If we didn't live in the same neighborhood, if she didn't know the neighborhood code, she'd have picked another friend who was cooler. I was sure of it. I did everything possible to keep Donna happy. Losing her as a friend would mean losing the other 'friends' at school who tolerated me because Donna told them to.

School didn't come easy for me. I studied hard for my honor roll grades. Mom wasn't sympathetic to this. She demanded good grades and found C's to be entirely unacceptable. When I earned a decent grade, I'd bring it to her as soon as I got off of the bus—beaming as she exclaimed how bright I was. I could almost hear her thinking it: *Ah ha! Something to brag to the neighbors about at the next block party.* But when I received bad grades, I hid them under my bed, threw them out on the bus, hid them in the bottom of my backpack, or threw them in the neighbors' bushes on my way home from school. I didn't want to disappoint her like I did myself, every day. I was tired of disappointment all around.

Donna and I were extremely excited one March day to learn that the fifth grade talent show was coming up. We rushed home that afternoon to begin working on our baton routine—one we were sure would steal the show. Her big sister, Christie, picked out the song we'd twirl to: "Freeze Frame". I'd never heard the song, but nodded as though I had. Donna, of course, knew all the words. We practiced our routine for months.

It was two days before the June talent show. Donna and I had our routine so well memorized I could run through it in my dreams. And I did dream about it. A lot. We marched on stage and proudly showed off tricks during the talent show dress rehearsal. I was glowing when I returned home. I was anxious to tell Mom—who, for as strict as she was, had always been my number one cheerleader—that our routine had been moved to the last. It was going to be the show stopper, I was sure of it. But my mother looked less than pleased. Her lips were pressed in a tight line. She glared at me with squinty hazel eyes, waiting for me to finish speaking. I finished, mid-sentence. Mom was sitting at the kitchen table, holding a piece of paper.

Why is she mad at me now? What did I do wrong? My stomach, including the Cheetos Donna and I had shared, flipped as I recognized the paper. It was the spelling test I'd hidden under my bed a week before. It was the spelling test I'd earned a 60 percent—an F—on. "What is *this*?" she screamed, shaking the spelling test at me. I winced, sure the neighbors could hear—again. *How is it possible this woman cares so much what the neighbors think but refuses to keep her voice down when she's screaming like a lunatic? Has she forgotten the neighborhood rules?*

Mom made no effort to lower her voice, convinced that the louder she yelled, the more fear I'd have. She was right. Two hours of lectures on hiding papers, a grounding, and a major headache later, I sat in my room too stunned to cry. I had to call Donna to let her know I was no longer allowed to participate in the following night's talent show and that she'd have to do the routine alone. I sat for at least an hour, afraid of what Donna would say. I wasn't nearly as upset about not being able to be in the talent show as I was in knowing that this could be what destroyed our fragile friendship. My instincts were correct.

Things were never the same between us. Donna resented me for "ruining" the talent show. She was even more hurt that I didn't come to cheer her on. She didn't understand how my mother could be. "It's only a sixty," she insisted. "Who cares? My brother gets sixties all the time and my parents don't care! Hell, I have three spelling tests under my bed right now and they don't even need to be there. I'm just too lazy to throw them away." Later, it was, "You aren't a true friend. You didn't even come to the show to watch me. You're just making up excuses about your mom. She's always nice to me. No one has rules like that. You're making it up…"

Donna was soon leading the kids in singing songs about me as I sat alone on the bus the following week. "Here comes Lisa, floatin' down the Delaware, chewin' on her underwear, can't afford another pair." The song beat at my brain as I tried to tune it out. The twenty-minute bus ride felt like it took hours. I reminded myself there was only three weeks left in the school year and hoped all would be forgotten by the time sixth grade rolled around. But, you guessed it, and I should have too: It wasn't.

Donna and I didn't play together that summer. We were placed in different classrooms for sixth grade. She soon had a new best friend, Lizzy, who didn't have rules or an "unreasonable mother" and who didn't "bail out on me." Lizzy, Donna reminded me, was a "true friend" and someone she could "count on." I didn't have the guts to ask Donna what kind of friend she thought she was. Instead, I told myself I didn't need Donna or her friendship.

I spent that summer playing with a girl across the street—one needier and nerdier than me. Lori, who was also four years younger than me, was the little sister I never had. She looked at me like I was Queen of Pine Street. She never argued and made me feel like maybe—just maybe—I was worth hanging out with. Mom asked why I didn't play with friends my own age. I shrugged and told her I "just don't feel like it". I wasn't interested in telling her how Lizzy and Donna had plans to go see the forbidden, rated PG-13, Madonna movie, "How Peggy Sue Got Married". I wasn't interested in telling her how Chris—whom I was not allowed to drive with—was driving them there. Instead, I tried to convince myself I didn't care. But I did. I cared a lot.

I spent the rest of my childhood pretending everything was alright. I earned good grades, continued to twirl my baton, took dance lessons, and spent as much time as I could alone in my bedroom sketching pictures and writing in a private journal marked "keep out" that Mom would later read. I liked being alone more and more. I also found better places to hide my bad grades. And I daydreamed, daily, of someday meeting a Farmer Charming.

***

Self-Diagnosis: Isolated.

96 Bottles: Loner Girl
"Early on, I learned to create my own worlds."

I stole bits of childhood contentment reading hundreds of books my godmother, Janie, sent me from the publishing firm she worked at. I loved those books, many of them under my reading level but perfectly suitable to my fetish for underdogs and all things happy ending. My favorites included *Ramona Quimby, Age 8,* and *Tales of a Fourth Grade Nothing.* Cuddled up on my lilac comforter, I hugged my Pound Puppies and Cabbage Patch Kids as I read of Ramona and Pippy Longstocking's impressive adventures and wondered if I'd ever live such a bold life.

Mom lured me to suppers each night in our cramped kitchen. There, cross-stitched signs read, "The Best Thing a Father Can Do for His Children is to Love Their Mother," "Home is Where the Heart Is," and "God Bless this Home." Dinner came with more rules. We were not allowed to eat until Dad got home from work—something that irritated my inner feminist more than the lining of my hungry stomach. Often this meant not eating until after eight. Second, we were not to start eating until we'd said grace. Lastly, we had to ask to be excused from the table before returning to whatever we were doing.

When our plates were clean, we routinely retreated to our favorite rooms in the house. For

Dad, this was the cellar. From work projects he tinkered with at home, to a train room he built under the dining room, Dad spent hours in the basement. One reason for this was because as we grew older, so did Mom's patience with his smoking. At some point, he was no longer allowed to smoke his Salem Menthols in the main house and was confined to the basement like a refugee. While I detested the smell of his smoke and the musty grime of the cellar, I often made my way downstairs to see what Dad was up to. He always welcomed me the same way; with a smile and a finger to his lips and a hushed, "Ssssh, don't tell your mother I'm smoking." *Like she doesn't know?* I kept his secret. I was good at secrets. Secrets were bad spelling tests tossed in dumpsters behind the school, never to be heard from again. If you could keep a secret successfully, you could maintain peace; the only thing I ever really wanted.

When I needed a friend, I marched across the street to Lori's house. Ever anxious to hang out with the cool older girl across the street, Lori was eager-eyed and happy to drop whatever she was doing to be with me. This pattern carried on throughout high school until we finally lost touch. Our daughter, Ella has a friend like this now, one who's younger and always happy to see her. I understand that. I don't question it. I don't ask her why she doesn't find friends her own age. She doesn't have a big sister, but she can play one to someone else. And that's good enough, for now.

***

Self-Diagnosis: A need to be needed, secret keeper. Future chain smoker.

95 Bottles: Birth of a Liar
"It was easier to fake a life than to actually live one."

My own Pippi-style adventure came when I was eleven. It was 1985 and I'd just finished sixth grade. An awkward, pimply mess who'd barely had her first period, my parents had great hopes that going away for two weeks might give me some confidence. My math teacher, a doughty but sweet woman named Mrs. Hoffman, worked summers as a counselor at Camp Hucklebee. She'd suggested the overnight camp to my parents at a late in the year parent conference.

Because Dad went to summer camp as a kid, my folks believed going to overnight camp stamped a child with a healthy sense of independence. "You need to know what it's like to be away from home," Mom said, helping me pick out a trunk to bring to camp. I dug my fingers deep in my pockets. Tears burned the back of my eyes. *If this is so important, why didn't you ever go?*

I shifted from one foot to the other, trying to find an excuse to cancel the prepaid camp adventure. *Maybe I should stay home and go to summer school so I can get better spelling grades. Who will feed Bubsey—my parakeet—while I'm gone?* For weeks I tried to come up with an out, but was unsuccessful. I had been keen on the idea of spending the summer with my neighborhood friends, hunting innocent salamanders and building hurricane-

45

proof forts. *Damn that parent conference.* A month later, instead of taking me up on my silent pleas for reprieve, Mom loaded me up with everything a camper could possibly need—plastic tins for late night runs to the makeshift wooden outhouses, flashlights for midnight storytelling and letter writing, and even the outlawed midnight *Snickers* bar.

The sixty miles to Chamberlaine, New Hampshire was torture. Dad hummed along with the radio while Mom reassured me, oh, three thousand times, of how much fun I was going to have. My brother Robbie sat beside me in our almond Buick with faux wooden paneling, smirking. I could hear him thinking, *Yeah, good luck with that, Sis! You're about to be ditched!* I wanted to reply, "Shut up, fucker. Your time is coming…" Instead I kept quiet, silently cursing my family and wishing I'd been born to people not so interested in getting rid of me: *Why couldn't I have been adopted? Maybe I am! Maybe my* real *parents would get that I am too chicken to really do this stuff! Who* are *these people?*

Later, I forced a courage-grin as my parents pulled away. *After all, the unheated, rustic cabin wasn't that bad. Didn't every girl want to sleep on the top bunk of a flimsy metal bed with ten strangers she didn't know? Wasn't it every girl's dream to trek half a mile into the woods in the middle of the night to shit in a urine-saturated hut? Yeah, this will be super. Thanks, Mom and Dad.*

I began the mental countdown to pick-up day before the Buick was out of sight. Inhaling like it was my last chance for oxygen, I hiked back to the cabin, praying the girls would be kinder than the ones at school. At least I'd have a chance to reinvent myself here. No one knew I was the butt of everyone's jokes back home. Hell, I didn't think my own family knew that. *Maybe this* would *be alright. Maybe.*

Somehow, I made it through my camp experience with my homesickness at bay, fears in check, and even a few sweet memories of innocent crushes on the boys at the nearby brother camp. When pick-up day arrived, I was oddly sentimental about the bug juice I'd miss and those long hikes to the bathroom with the crickets. Sensing I'd survived, and taking this as a sign I'd successfully handle the mandatory college experience, my parents were more than chipper on the drive home. Dad let me sing every camp song I'd learned, replacing the words with his own. He cheerfully navigated the windy trip, while successfully sucking down about twenty cigarettes. I sat in the backseat, eyes shut, humming. *Maybe all I needed was a little space and time away from my hometown. No one had to know that, while there, I'd invented a new persona for myself.*

Back home, I told them, I was the most popular girl in school. "All the guys like me. I just don't know who I like best," I'd told the girls in my cabin. *God forbid they find out I couldn't even score a date with Napoleon Dynamite if I paid him.* "Kissing boys? Ha! I've done that a thousand times. It's no biggie," I'd laughed, flipping my hair like Ginger on "Gilligan's Island.". "You *haven't* kissed a boy? Geesh!" I became a good storyteller that summer. I had even myself believing I'd really kissed ten boys. I could see their lips and the look in their eyes as they took me behind the play-ground tire swings to make out with my ravishing self. I stole from the lives and recess gossip of the popular girls and made their experiences my own. I'm not sure if a writer or a liar was born there. Probably a little bit of both. But oddly enough? It worked. They all believed me. *Camp was okay! Maybe, someday, I'd have a chance to do it again. But next time, maybe—just maybe—I could just be me. And someone would like me for the real me—maybe.*

***

Self-Diagnosis: Dreamer. Storyteller.

94 Bottles: Keeping Secrets
"Your secret's safe with me."

Given my insecurities, newly acquired knack for telling tales—okay, blatant lies in the name of ego preservation—and strict 80s upbringing, it was no surprise that I felt an innate need to hide the troubles Jeff and I were having in our marriage from beer one. It's one thing to be frowned upon as a child, but it's completely humiliating for this particular adult. I should have been used to not measuring up, but I wasn't. In fact, my relationship with Jeff got me frowns pretty much from the beginning.

My premarital pregnancy with JJ set my mother into a three-week-shotgun-wedding-planning-frenzy and brought back familiar worries of, "What will the neighbors think?" The one brides-maid dress for my wedding—worn by Amy, my college roommate and childhood friend—was plucked off the rack of a thrift shop last minute on a January afternoon to match the poinsettia flowers that would already be at the church leftover from the holiday season. "Be practical, Lisa," Mom warned when I pleaded with her to stick to my original lilac theme and May wedding date. I hate the color red almost as much as I hate winter. But this wasn't up to me. Her eyes answered me and I knew better than to argue. "This. Is. How. It's. Going. To. Be." *No wedding the way I want it for me. No wedding shower either. Those things are for girls who follow the rules.* When you don't follow the rules, there are punishments. Again, I should have known better. Apparently, I'm not a quick learner.

For the most part, I didn't care. I spent my nights talking to the tiny baby growing inside of me. People all around us weren't shy about voicing their doubts that Jeff and I would ever work. At our wedding they made bets about how long we'd last and whispered in corners about my budging waistline. A decade later, to give my parents more reason to doubt me or my decisions? It wasn't going to happen. No, Jeff's drinking secret would stay safe with me—just like my summer camp alter ego—until I just couldn't hold it in any longer.

I also feared that, Mom, in particular, would offer her famous saying: "My heart bleeds for you", if I told my family about Jeff. Mom threw this phrase out like rice at a wedding throughout my childhood. She was so fond of it, in fact, that she actually sang it: "My heart bleeeeeeeds for you, my heart bleeeeeeeeeds for you!" she'd chirp in her happiest singing voice. I'd sit in the back of the car gritting my teeth, trying to tune her out. Translation of this particular chorus? "Get over it, you're being a baby and making a big deal out of nothing."

As a teen, I announced to Mom that I'd never say those words to my children. I'm proud to report that I have kept that promise. I've also kept my vow never to cook meatloaf for my children. Some family cycles, it seems, *can* be broken. Regardless, the last thing I could hear in regards to my marriage was, "My heart bleeds for you." And so, for years, I didn't even hint at any problems in my personal life. They would remain just that, personal.

***

My therapist, a woman who I nicknamed Quaker Oates—for her incessant need to try to get me to start attending services in her Quaker religion—is staring at me. I know she's disappointed I didn't turn in my last two sessions' homework assignments. Today, I don't care. *Isn't Jeff the one who should be in therapy? I'm just along for the ride, Oates.* She thinks she's being slick when she glances up at a clock tucked behind a wall quilt behind my head. She's unaware of my ability to take in surroundings fast because of my journalism training. I don't call her on her bluff. I know there has to be at least forty minutes left to this session, which seems to be running at a slug's pace.

Finally conceding that I do, in fact, communicate more naturally through writing than conversation, Quaker has given me an assignment to write about a time when I made a deliberate change in my life, why I made that change, and how it has changed my life. While I haven't put it on paper, I did come armed with an answer for her today. I offer it to her in concession.

"When I had JJ, the day he was born, he had the most amazing curls. I knew he got them from me. The first time I held him, I remember thinking that he was mine. He was all mine. That's when I started to cry," I explain. "The first time I held him I was only twenty-one. I told him—out loud—that I was sorry I was his mother. He was too good for me and I felt like I didn't deserve such a precious gift. Part of me wanted to give him up because I felt like he'd been robbed in the whole parent-picking raffle. By the time Ella came around, I felt the same about her, but for different reasons. No little girl deserves a drunk for a father."

Quaker jumps from her seat faster than I've ever seen her 300-plus-pound frame move. She leans forward on her elbows, eying me like I am about to have a therapeutic breakthrough. She says nothing. Wanting to please, I continue.

"Anyway, it was later that first night, in the hospital with JJ...Jeff was asleep on a crappy couch they had for him and I was alone with my newborn son. It was the first time I changed his diaper. I was alone with this amazing creature. I made a promise to him and to myself that I'd find a way to get my life together and be the best mother I could possibly be. I told him I'd do everything I could to be sure he had a loving, happy home and that he'd always be able to come to me," I say. "I wanted him to know I would be the kind of mom who he could talk to and that he wasn't afraid of. I promised to never jump into rages or judge him before hearing his side of the story. I promised to always defend and protect him and to make him my priority in all things. I made the same promise to my other two, too."

"Do you feel like you've done that?" Quaker's voice startles me, pulling me out of my monologue.

"Yes. Mostly," I say.

"Mostly? Want to elaborate?"

I nod. "Well, I'm a great mother. I don't think many good things about myself, but what I do know for sure is that I am a good mom. I am there for the kids in everything they do. They aren't afraid to talk to me. I very rarely yell at them. I've never hit them. Ella adores me, probably Jeff more, but that's a Daddy's girl kind of thing. They know they can talk to me. I don't freak out about the little things. They trust me. And they know I love them no matter what."

"That's all pretty important stuff that not all parents can say," Quaker says. "You should feel proud of that. What made you make those promises to your son—to all of your kids?"

"I remember what it was like to be a kid. I remember not knowing if I was coming or going. I'd get in huge trouble for the tiniest thing and no trouble at all for a super huge thing," I said. "I never felt safe, emotionally, I mean."

"Do you feel safe now?"

"You mean with Jeff? Or with my parents?"

"Both."

I laugh, knowing I should never give Quaker an option for more. She's like a greedy sponge. *I wonder if she's a reality TV junkie too? She thrives on this shit. Her husband is probably a coke addict and her father a schizophrenic.*

"That's the thing. Believe it or not, with Jeff, I *do* feel very secure emotionally. I know, it's crazy. I feel safe with a drunk. Great. But he's listened to my issues, helped me through many of them, and I know what to expect with him. Even when he drinks or gets bitchy—which we both know is constant—I feel like it's predictable. As a kid, I craved anything I could count on. I needed to know people's reactions before they happened. When I couldn't predict them, I chose to lie or in some way manipulate those reactions," I say. I pause, my thoughts coming too fast. *Damn, I may actually be having a therapeutic break through here. Damn Quaker!* "...I still don't know if my parents are coming or going. I don't understand many of the things they do. Worse, I don't understand why, at my age, I care."

"Is that what makes you stay? Is knowing what to expect why it's easier for you to stay than leave your marriage?"

"No. Because ultimately nothing is more unpredictable than how this will all end. What makes me stay is knowing I belong somewhere. For the first time in my life, I feel like I belong. I belong with Jeff and my three children," I sigh, letting tears flow down my cheeks until Quaker calls it early quits for the day. Guilt overwhelms me. "That wasn't anyone's fault. My peers hated me. And you try growing up with no sisters, all brothers, and being totally misunderstood. My father's answer for everything was, "It's her hormones," and, "Ignore her, she's a girl."

"Good work. Now we're getting somewhere."

"Yeah. Great," I say, grabbing extra tissues for the seven-minute ride home. *Therapy sucks.*

***

Self-Diagnosis: Needy with a preference for denial. Still a slow learner.

93 Bottles: Boy Crazy Me
"They say that addicts attract addicts. I've been a love addict since age twelve."

My first romantic feelings for a boy came by way of Jonathan McGovern. Jon was a relatively popular kid. What I found intriguing about him was that he was nice to everyone, even the plankton of the social chain. Jon was an artist. He drew candid portraits and wore baggy sweatshirts and jeans; something that wasn't in style at the time. He was not afraid to be himself and I admired that. Jon was the type of kid who could go to summer camp and just be himself, no lies needed.

Jon knew I had feelings for him. Clarification: Primates in other countries and time zones knew I had feelings for him. My notebooks screamed it with hearts and "Lisa Loves Jon 4eva's!" A kind soul, he gracefully bowed out with the whole, "I'm not old enough to date" line that I now teach my own sons. Not able to take even the kindest of rejections well, I chased him around the playground with Amy, taking numerous pictures of him. I was persistent at minimum. They'd refer to my behavior as stalking by today's standards. I even handed my camera over to the now acquaintance-only-when-convenient-because-you're-still-not-forgiven-for-the-talent-show Donna, who had more classes with him, to see if she could get a better shot. She did. (Of his ass.)

Things never went anywhere with Jon. I am quite sure he was flattered by my interest in him, but certainly was not interested in me. Hollywood stars love the paparazzi when they first hit platinum, but eventually being chased with cameras and swooned over gets old even for guys like George Clooney.

After being rejected by Jon, I lowered my standards in eighth grade. By then, I'd been diagnosed with asthma and was the poster child for antihistamines. That, combined with my white girl's afro and already 5'6 scrawny frame were enough to send any boy running in the other direction. Queen-of-Phlegm-and-All-Things-Inhaler, I set my sights on a seventh grader named Tim Smith. Tim was as bland as his name. If I was plankton, Tim was zooplankton. Ever the optimist, I looked for his positives: His deep green eyes and the way he over-used Polo cologne were his calling cards. Pathological masochist that I was, I asked Tim to meet me at a school Valentine's Day dance. My mother bought me a special Valentine's Day sweatshirt with silver glitter hearts across the chest. Tonight would be perfect. I was sure of it. Maybe even tonight would be my first kiss.

I was dancing with him close, feeling sorry for and somehow above the girls sitting in the bleachers when I realized I forgot to put deodorant on. I didn't just hint at smelling bad: I *reeked*. I was the picture of puberty in its rawest form and we both knew it. I couldn't even look at him and was nearly as relieved as he was when the song ended. He didn't ask me to dance again and I spent the rest of the night in the bleachers with a girlfriend, listening to songs like "Faithfully" by Journey. I was faithfully heartbroken.

I gave up on boys for about a year after Tim. A girl could only take so much and I decided they weren't worth the disappointment. I was convinced no guy would ever want to be with me anyway. By then I was about three inches taller than any of the boys in my school, pimples bulged from what seemed like every pore on my face, and my social confidence had plunged deeper than the ocean floor. This was how I entered high school: *You. Aren't. Shit.*

But I was not entirely without a plan. Girls who write daily in journals have a lot of time for self-pep talks and list making. And so, I talked myself up for the entire summer prior to high school. I stocked up on deodorant, got contact lenses, and convinced Mom to let me get a perm. High school seemed like a place of new opportunities. Initially, I welcomed the new faces and the hope that maybe one of the taller boys would take pity on me and I could somehow start over. The thing about growing up in the same town and never moving is that you can never fully reinvent yourself. If you start out as an awkward kid, chances are, no matter how much you work to improve your social graces or out of date hairstyle, you're still going to be that same misfit at the end of the day.

Hope came my freshman year in the form of a new student transplant, Jeff Gagne. I now like to refer to him as Jeff, version 1.0. Jeff was a tall blonde with gorgeous blue eyes who had a thing for tall girls. He was smart and engaging. I liked him instantly. I took him under my wing—showing him around the school and introducing him to new people. Upon learning about his interests in art and writing, I brought him my favorite book on Disney cartooning. I left notes for him in his locker. I waited for him after classes. I talked to him on the phone at night. I did whatever I could to keep him interested in me.

This time, it worked. It was at my high school's homecoming dance in 1988 that I had my first kiss, dancing to Def Leppard's "Love Bites". Jeff wore a teal and white striped shirt, one that made his ocean eyes pop. He had on just the right amount of Polo. And I, of course, had layered on the Secret. I was amused by the obvious erection he had as we danced close and he moved in for that kiss. Unsure, I let him take the lead and was instantly addicted to the feel of being held by a guy. I allowed him to put his hands low on my waist, before they slid down to my ass, as we danced and made out. Someone told us to, "Get a room." I finally belonged. I know: Pathetic.

Things didn't last long with Jeff. Enter Kristi Tanner. Kristi was a bug-eyed brunette with the personality of a toad, but she was a shark in the food chain simply by virtue of living next door to the most popular girl in school. Kristi was popular because she was best friends with Marianne Marsh. It turns out that it was actually Marianne that Jeff was interested in. I took great joy in watching him later be rejected by Marianne for not being popular enough himself.

Regardless, early and repeat rejections by boys left me turning inward, back to my fantasy world where I dreamed of what my Farmer Charming would be like. Jeff 2.0, the upgrade, would never hurt me with words and would actually believe I was beautiful. He wouldn't mind my coarse hair, my pimples, my clumsy nature, or my awkward way of being with people—particularly when I was nervous. I often made lists in my journals of what this imaginary man would be like. For some reason, I thought he'd be named Bill. I had a very vivid fantasy of making love with Bill on the floor by a fireplace and sipping wine afterwards. He was always barefoot in this fantasy and had very sexy toes. I do not, nor did I ever, have a foot fetish, but for some reason, his feet stuck with me. Farmer Charming would make good money—enough for me to stay home with the kids while they were young—and a big appetite. He'd love to come home to the dinners I'd make for him, always appreciative of the love I'd put into them. I'd be a great writer, working from home when I wasn't at PTA meetings or other events for the children. I envisioned my mother's life, but better. Somehow, I'd have more love and passion than she'd had. My husband would never sleep in late on the weekends, missing church. And I certainly wouldn't ever marry a man who'd call dishes "woman's work" or nickname our only daughter "Kelly Bundy" after a slutty sitcom character on "Married with Children".

These days, it's Ella who is boy crazy. It makes me nuts listening to her. I wish I could fill her head with all my experiences, but I can do nothing. I understand, now, why Mom had her rules. She was only trying to protect me. But I worry that rules—too many or too harsh—will only push Ella away from me. I listen silently, stalking teenage boys late at night on Facebook to make sure they won't hurt my little girl. I've learned, you can't protect them. Not really. No matter how hard you try. We do talk, though, about Jeff's drinking and how she won't marry a man who drinks. I hope she really means it. She seems to think it's okay for him—her Daddy and the first man she's ever loved—to do it. It's just not for her own Farmer Charming.

I tell Ella she doesn't need a man at all. She laughs at me, asking why, if I've never left Dad, would I even say such a thing. She's wise for her years. "Mom, we only get what we're willing to accept. You are okay with Dad the way he is and so am I, for a father," she says. "I just won't marry a guy like that. Everything else, like Dad, but not the drinking." Somehow, I believe her. It's probably my denial. Again. Or maybe it's my hope that by giving her a place to talk about it she really has thought it through.

***

Self-Diagnosis: Love addict, through and through. In love with dreams of happy endings. Also? Horrible version of a feminist. Shame on me. Hot mess. Obsessed with deodorant permanently.

92 Bottles: My First Beer
"If everyone has a price, mine was acceptance."

My cousin Dan and I are only a few weeks apart. Dan's a big guy, about 6'2 and well over 220 pounds of solid muscle. His personality matches the thick red afro he keeps trimmed tight on his oval head. Dan's the type of guy whose voice can be heard easily three rooms away, whether at a family gathering at his family home or walking into your grandfather—Red's—funeral. I've always admired this—the way he stirs laughter and a welcome feeling in the hearts of those around him.

As teens, Dan took pride—God only knows why, maybe his parents were paying him—in dragging my four-eyed self to and from various social events in his popular crowd. One night, after telling Aunt Debbie he was taking me to the movies and asking her for $40, I found myself at a party hosted by his skinny friend, Chuck. Chuck was a cute boy, if you're into skinny boys—which I'm not—and don't mind the preppy look. I had met him before at one of Dan's basketball games but had written him off as "not my type". (As if Chuck would have even considered lowering himself to my pond scum social status level).

Snobby would be an understatement for Chuck. I was quite sure he ironed his gym socks after a good starching. But Chuck was always nice to me. He had to be. Dan's eyes told him to be.

We couldn't have been in his parent's elaborate bay-side cape for more than a minute before Chuck graciously handed me an ice cold can of Budweiser. He gulped his down extra fast. Wide-eyed, I wondered if he would get a brain freeze. I'd never tasted booze before. The closest I'd come was bringing them to and from my grandfather during his bi-monthly Friday night visits with my parents. I stared at the deranged liquid from another planet and was relieved it wasn't the kind of bottle you needed a special device I knew nothing about to open. Dan came to my rescue, popping his beer open and gulping down a big sip. I followed his lead. This was mistake number one. Everything in me wanted to spit it right back out. I had an instant brain freeze, the kind I'd had many times before with Slush Puppies from the 7-Eleven in my hometown. I wasn't sure I remembered how to swallow but managed to do it anyway.

Three beers, a rookie introduction to the game of quarters, and two Jello shots later, swallowing was no problem at all. Dave was off with a girl in Chuck's parents' room and Chuck and I were already at his bed. I don't know how I got there, but I was quite impressed at how he'd managed to do it. *God, he's skinny. Freakishly skinny.* He laid across his bed, slowly unbuttoning the top three buttons of his aqua polo shirt. Next went his jeans. I stared at him for a moment, even considered making a joke about how he should eat something, and got to the business of doing what I was there for. *Awkward.*

Ten minutes later, buttoning his jeans, he stood up abruptly and announced, "You comin'?"

"Yeah, sure, um, what year are your trophies from? They're nice," I stalled, wanting any excuse to feel like we'd actually connected on some level deeper than the sperm pool in my stomach. And definitely not interested in returning from the basement in such a quick time period—that'd only say one of two things: either, she puts out quick, or she's a prude. I don't know which would have been worse.

I'd never have made it home that night if it weren't for Dan's experience with partying and drunk driving. Somehow, we did make it back to his parent's house and the rest of the night was a blur. I was glad to return to my hometown the following morning, where people only knew me as the dorky girl, not the town slut. And certainly not the girl who spent the night throwing up in a stranger's toilet. *Nope, alcohol is not for me,* I told myself.

***

Self-Diagnosis: Low self-esteem and self-worth. No boundaries. "That" girl. Young. Naive.

91 Bottles: Turning Inward
"Broken faucet, broken dreams."

You can't understand the loneliness of being married to an alcoholic unless you've been there. On sober days, I am married to a wonderful person, my best friend, with whom I share normal hopes and dreams. On drinking nights, that man disappears and is replaced by someone I only regretfully recognize. He becomes a sloppy, sometimes angry, sometimes an overly mushy "thing". I began referring to him, my once-dreamy-cowboy-wannabe-farmer-charming, during these times, as "the Night Crawler" to Mr. Journal. In my journal, I scratched out hate poems about him as he stumbled through the kitchen looking for late-night snacks:

Night Crawler

Creeping around in the dark
the sound of saran wrap eats at me
like the food it shields
from his greedy lips.

I jump to the sound of the ice tray
doing its best
to pour frozen promises
from a broken faucet.
Broken dreams.

99 Bottles

ERIN LEE

I wonder:
Does aluminum foil make less noise?
Tip toeing lighter than his high
to dig deep into the back
for food I've cooked
but he'll complain about.

I exhale to the taste
of moldy expectations
and a faucet
run frigid.

I muse:
At least there's something to write about?
Please! Go away! Night crawler bug
who trips over carpet lint
and makes my skin itch.

Go back to your cave,
night crawler bug!
Do you know:
Broken souls are contagious?

I itch.
And I sigh:
The kids have never brought home head lice.
My ears, open wide,
listening for the night crawler
and wondering:
For how much longer?

99 Bottles   ERIN LEE

While writing what I referred to as "hate poetry" about Jeff's drinking helped to sooth my frustrations, I was still quite cognoscente of the fact that marriage is a two-way street. Oates helped me realize that I came to Jeff with enough emotional baggage for six lifetimes, complete with a carry-on of insecurities, wounds, and Xanax. For that reason, I began to take a closer look at myself when the glass got too grimy to be shining the bright lights on him. (I've never been big on housecleaning anyway.)

I've always believed the way a couple sleeps says a lot about their relationship. When I crawl into bed, Jeff still reaches for me and holds me close, careful not to put too much weight on my lungs. After five minutes, I roll over, cupping his firm stomach in my left hand. Our legs entwined, he allows me to warm my night-chilled feet on his hamstrings. We've slept this way for years. Settled into the idea that we are polar opposites, we are content with the routine we have cultivated over our nearly two decades together. A morning person, I depend on him as an alarm clock for days when the kids need me up before school. At night, he sleeps easier knowing I am awake and will wake him if there is a problem in the house. We've defined our roles so clearly that we no longer fight about who will do laundry—him—and who will attend parent conferences—me. He is stern, disciplined, and serious. I am carefree, sloppy, and good-natured. Queen of Denial, I am able to put problems in the back of my mind, while he fixates on balancing the checkbook to the penny. If bills

67

were up to me, I would be lucky to note half the checks I wrote in the register and escape without bounce fees for a month.

In spite of our differences, we sit in comfortable silences and laugh at the same jokes. I let his temper tantrums fly unquestioned. He wakes up in the middle of the night to pound on my back during asthma attacks or to get me medicine. He sleeps with my inhaler in his hand, ready at any moment to force feed it to me. It's in our silent routines that we are bound. Our natural rhythm replaces the passion we once shared, but is somehow more intimate. He reads the sign language of my eyebrows like other people read *Cliff's Notes*. And I own the *Farmer's Almanac* to his moods.

***

Self-Diagnosis: Comfortable. Maybe too comfortable.

90 Bottles: Patterns
"Could we get a break in the rain?"

While the stories of the men and women I've en-
countered in Alanon meetings are each unique, it
wasn't long into meetings that I realized they pos-
sess similarities too. Namely, when people speak
of their alcoholics, they speak of patterns.

By late 2002, my husband's pattern of alcohol
abuse was as easy to predict as my infant
daughter's sleeping and eating patterns. How this
surprised me, given his love of all things routine
and predictability in other aspects of life, is beyond
me. A man who believes the color yellow—my
favorite—is a risk is not about to operate differently when it comes to his addiction. Instead, he will
invariably choose to construct a routine around his
binges.

By then, Jeff was working full time as a lead
carpenter. He'd come home from work three times
a week with a six-pack of Budweiser Ice at 4 p.m.
My job allowed me to be home in the afternoons
after JJ was out of kindergarten for the day. I'd
pick JJ up from school, get Nathan and Ella from
daycare, and begin cooking supper.

Our dinner schedule was one of the first things to
revolve around Jeff's drinking. He'd announced,
somewhere in those early years, that he was no
longer going to eat dinner on "drinking nights".
Eating food, he reasoned, prevented him from
getting drunk as quickly. And, since I was

"micromanaging" the amount of beers he consumed, he felt he had to be sure he got the best buzz he could get off that six-pack. With him drinking every other night, I adapted to cooking the kids' favorite meals on his drinking nights. Chicken fingers, Sheppard's pie, hot dogs, and hamburgers on the grill became staples for us on those nights. On sober nights, we ate Jeff's favorites; manicotti, lasagna, and chicken parm. There was a part of me, on those sober nights, that felt like if I made dinners happier, made him feel more special, he'd somehow want to be sober. That was only one mistake in the hundreds I made as I began my long journey as the wife of an alcoholic. I just didn't know it yet.

I often wonder if I should have paid more attention to the dullness in his eyes. They carried the hardness of a lifelong drinker by the time he was thirty. When he'd come home at night, he'd force a smile at me, tilting his head. His expression reminded me of an undertaker and his arms would lay listless at his sides as I said my hellos and debated asking him how his day went. Doing so would generate a twenty-minute bitch fest about the state of the economy or the $4 cost of milk. Eventually, I stopped asking and retreated into a self-induced fantasyland where Farmer Charming's smiles were real and he hugged me back.

I'm not sure if it was the drinking or the depression that came first to begin this pattern. Jeff told me early on that he'd suffered from depression as a child. I'd thought very little of it. Blinded by love, I didn't understand how difficult depression could be—not only to the person suffering from it, but to the people who loved that person. I also viewed his mood swings as another layer to his depth that I so admired. But I soon noted a fragile tango between Jeff's depression and drinking: He'd get down and would use beer to self-medicate.

Living with his moods was almost as difficult as living with his drinking. He'd swing into rants the kids and I would refer to as "Dad's rages". During these times, we knew our best bet was to stay as far away from him as possible. While he never hit us, he became skilled at using his voice, body language, and sudden outbursts to control us with fear. Intentionally or not, these sober rages often made me rush to hand him the bottle—if only to calm him down: Just another part of our dance. I became unsure of who was leading.

***

May, 2010

Jeff and I decide to go to Buffalo for a trip to our favorite bookstore. He's looking for a book on Holstein dairy cows. He has a gift card from his birthday. I'm fidgety lately and want some new reading material. It's about eighty degrees and the air conditioner in our used pickup truck is broken. Despite the humidity and heat, we're having a pleasant conversation about books and current events. When the conversation shifts to JJ's upcoming soccer camp and Ella's new daycare, his mood also switches. I was recently laid off from my job as an entertainment editor at the local paper. It's the first time in our marriage where I'm not contributing financially, aside from a meager unemployment check. With finances strained, he's furious when I tell him about the increased childcare rate and $100 camp fee due that coming Wednesday. He peels out of the parking lot, making a scene as he speeds down the road. I offer to take the kids out of daycare until I get a new job to save money. He ignores me. Knowing that saying anything more will only fuel his anger, I keep my mouth shut—trying to contain my carsickness. And what began as a nice afternoon together quickly turns into a silent, dangerous ride home.

Car rides like these were frequent throughout most of our marriage. In March of 2006, Jeff bought a sports car. This car was the fastest sports car on the market for under $60,000. His pride and joy, he delighted in taking the family on rides where he'd put the petal to the metal and see how quickly he could get from zero to sixty miles per hour. While the boys squealed in delight, Ella and I clenched our teeth. I clung to the passenger's side door handle. Sometimes, I asked him to slow down. Most times, I sat, lips pressed tight, and silently counting the minutes for the ride to be over. I often reached behind me, to rub Ella's leg; a silent reassurance she never really fell for.

Car rides and dinner menus weren't the only things that began to hug Jeff's drinking and mood schedules. Bedtimes, sleeping arrangements, and family time all wrapped themselves around his sobriety or lack of it. Always a pleaser, I tried to roll with these changes without giving him much grief. I'd find little ways to compromise with him; encouraging him to help us with the jack-o-lanterns early so he'd still have time for "relaxing"—read: drinking—was a way of keeping him involved with the kids without conflict. *They need a father,* I told myself, unsure they really did.

***

Jeff isn't the only one with patterns in our household. The perfect yin to his yang, I surrender to nightly routines that comfort me like old friends or the tennis shoes in my closet from my glory days as executive editor of the college newspaper. When the beer's gone and he's retreated to our bedroom, I make my first cup of tea. I settle in on my warm spot on the couch—fitted perfectly to my growing ass—and reach for the remote. A reliable friend, I use the remote to program six hours of television sure to make me feel better about my life. Reality television does the trick. There's "Hoarders," "Intervention," "16 and Pregnant," "Teen Mom," "Obese and Pregnant," and "The Secret Lives of Women" to make a woman feel better about her own problems.

Tonight's episode of "Hoarders" features a woman being forced to leave her home because of her obsession with birds and clutter. Afraid of being hurt, the woman has built a shield around her by creating a home no one can visit. This reminds me of a recent book I read, *Dry,* by Augustine Burrows. In this book, he describes coming home from treatment for alcoholism to an apartment so cluttered with empty bottles that it's unlivable. He writes of gathering the empty bottles, swarming with bugs, and filling dozens and dozens of trash bags with them. I imagine what would happen if I stopped clearing Jeff's bottles off the counter and began letting them accumulate. At nine cans a night, it would only take ten days before there would literally be 99 cans on my counter tops. In a year, there'd be 3,285. In five, 16,425 empty beer cans would overtake our modest home. While I'm at the math anyway—never my strong suit—at five cents a can, I figure the town recycling plant has made over $850 on my husband's habit since we moved to town in 2004. *It's a good thing we aren't hoarders. I wonder if the town will get that playground building project going soon. They certainly have our share of the seed money for it.*

As I calculate these figures with one eye on the bird lady and sip my tea, I hear him pop open another can in the bedroom. This shouldn't surprise me. He generally has a spare. Like chain smokers who stash an extra pack in their glove compartments in case of an emergency, I've learned that alcoholics take special care to keep their supplies full. The type of man to buy two extra cases of paper towels any time he goes grocery shopping "just because it makes me feel better," Jeff is no different about his beer. But tonight, the pop makes me jump and fills me with something I haven't often felt—indifference.

Indifference is not part of my usual self-pitying eat-til-you-feel-better,   crazy-like-me-bitch-to-your-journal, drown-your-feelings-in-reality-TV daily habit. The awkwardness of it makes me want to dive head first into Nathan's stash of left over Halloween Hershey candy bars. I resist. *Quaker Oates*—who also happens to be morbidly obese—*told you to sit with your feelings. To let yourself get uncomfortable. Oprah says don't eat your feelings, feel them. Jesus. Someone shoot me. Does anyone care that he's in there, right this second, drinking his feelings? I wonder how his liver feels about that?... Stop it. It's not your problem. It's not worth the empty calories and the heart condition and diabetes. The kids are already looking at a father with impending cirrhosis. Save them the grief and change the pattern, idiot. Ella is watching you.*

***

Self-Diagnosis: Self-loathing.

89 Bottles: No, Thanks!
"Orientation day: Dress rehearsal to disaster."

Graduating from, and more importantly, leaving high school was no great loss for me. I skip-marched across the stage to accept my diploma. The only thing shining brighter than my smile that day was the handmade yellow bus on my mortarboard. The bus was a tribute to my best friend Amy. For years, we'd argued about where it was we'd actually met in the first grade—on a summer school bus or in the playground. I was convinced it was the bus. She was certain it was the playground.

One of my best friends since the first grade, minus the year or two that I hung out with Donna, Amy had suffered a birth injury that left her with a half paralyzed left arm. It was because of her cast that she seemed so approachable to ultra-shy me when I met her. I was enamored by her outgoing personality and wit. Amy was the only thing good about high school, as far as I was concerned, and I didn't have to worry about leaving her behind.

Armed with an arsenal of reasons why it'd be "super" and "awesome" to go to college an hour from home together, I'd convinced the more socially adventurous Amy to be my college roommate. Bound not for the big city or to see the world for the first time with our own eyes, Amy, my 1988 Plymouth Reliant called Bertha 1.0, and I would head off to college entirely intact. I made sure of it. I was armed with a first-hand inspected list of who was bringing the forbidden dorm room hot pot and color coordinated twin bunk comforters. There was no great mystery or adventure there—just the way I'd ordered it. Ames was my very own human security blanket, disguised as a seventeen-year-old college coed, with a waist smaller than mine, tits bigger than mine, and confidence that could fill an empty atrium. Her ruby lips never grew tired of talking and her sharp mind always knew just what to say. Yes, I was going to be just fine with Amy at the helm, I decided.

See you pricks later! I blew a kiss to my graduating class of 248 and told myself I'd "show them" come my ten-year reunion where I'd emerge as a famous journalist. By then, I'd have seen the world and written not one, but three books about my adventures as a foreign correspondent. I'd have ridden in Air Force bomber jets alongside my Tom Cruise fighter pilot (someday to turn farmer when it was time to settle down) fiancé who adored me, and only me. *Who'd have to know that I'd likely need to pack trusty Amy in my suitcase to help me out of sticky situations along the way?*

It wasn't more than a few hours into our first day at college that my romantic notions of following my best childhood friend to college fell flat. I'm not talking about the kind of flat you can pump right back up. I'm talking about the kind of life halt that makes you choke on usually fresh air—like smog from a faulty exhaust.

99 Bottles

ERIN LEE

Our mothers, eager to participate in the freshmen welcoming activities set up for Orientation Weekend, were heading to a Class of 1996 welcoming reception in the school gymnasium. Somehow, the ever-clever Amy convinced them we needed to do a few things before meeting back up with them. Amy encouraged them to go ahead of us, and assured our moms we'd be right along. Puzzled, but well-versed in the oh-so-slick ways of my hero-friend, I went along with this. Mom and Mrs. D were off to the reception alone before I had a chance to look back at them. They'd barely rounded the corner of the grassy quad before Amy pulled at my arm—hard.

"Come on! We don't have much time, dude! Are you really going to wear *that*?" She pulled me behind our dorm, Fiske Hall, and frantically searched through her oversized Benneton bag for something.

"Huh? What's wrong with what I'm wearing?" I looked down at my Planet Earth t-shirt and black jeans. My feet topped off what I considered a perfectly invisible, perfectly please-don't-stare-at-me-isn't-it-obvious-I'm-petrified? outfit paired with my lucky Ked sneakers.

Amy was already moving quickly along the edge of the dorm, eyes set on something across the street.

"Dude! Wait! Where are we going? What are you...?"

"Ah-ha! Here!" She stopped, finally, and stripped out of her acid washed jeans. She threw them in the bag, revealing Daisy Duke hot shorts in a startling crisp white. These were the kind of shorts I'd imagined seeing in a go-go bar. These were the kind of shorts no girl over the age of twelve would consider wearing for fear that her period may come and announce its presence just a little too loudly. I'd never seen these shorts before and I was quite sure I had a full inventory of all of Amy's clothes. *Didn't we just do a full wardrobe inventory before bed last night?* No, I was quite sure I'd never seen these before. I'd have remembered the way they split her ass cheeks and cupped them awkwardly—like two overflowing cupcakes someone's mother would donate to a school fundraiser. My jaw hung as she twirled around behind the dorm, throwing cherry lipstick my way. The lipstick landed on the sidewalk.

I looked around, sure we must have an audience, before reaching to pick it up off the walkway. We did, indeed, have an audience. Looking up, across the street, I spotted at least a half dozen older boys—*juniors, maybe?*—on the roof of a slummy building. The boys were sitting on a row of ratty couches, sporting Budweiser cans and people watching. To say Amy-watching would probably be more appropriate here.

"There! " she said, grinning, and pretending to be oblivious to the scene she was stirring, "We're all set! Let's go! "

Amy looked up at the boys, but only after Indian-grabbing the lipstick from my palm and applying what must have been a fourth or fifth coat to her well-oiled lips. I froze. Vomit, acid, the two percent milk I'd had with my cereal that morning, whatever was in my stomach, seemed to want to make a reappearance. And it wanted to do it all over the walkway. *Why not?* I facetiously reasoned. *It's not like a major puking incident would ruin the lipstick job I've apparently forgotten—or wasn't fast enough to get to.*

Amy was already marching through the crosswalk like a Cheshire cat on speed to the rotting sage Victorian. To say she was moving quickly is an understatement. No, her and her slut shorts were most definitely doing a speed-walk, enunciated by the tit-buns that matched her cupcakes as she belly danced toward the boys. I had no choice but to vomit or follow. I did as I always did. Like the homeless puppy dog I often felt like, I obediently raced to catch up to my crazy owner. *So much for dragging her along for the ride…*

"Cool!" I offered, a little too convincingly. "Do you *know* them?"

Amy's older brother, Paul, whom I'd had a not-so-secret crush on for years, was already a sophomore. I reasoned, quite lamely, with myself, that this could just be an innocent, "let's stop in and say hi to Paul" visit. I soon discovered that it was, indeed, a "let's see Paul" visit. But that was only the cover story. No different than the "we just have a few things to do real quick" excuse she'd told our moms, Amy's "let's go see Paul" idea was more of a teaser on the cover of a tabloid; complete with a promise of something juicier inside. I didn't have to wait long to get to the guts of the story behind my newly discovered centerfold of a best friend. I followed Amy through the open front door of the house with dingy Greek letters on it.

The first thing I noticed was the acidic cocktail of piss and beer that permeated the walls and flooring of the building. I'd have bet those walls hadn't been painted since it was built in 1909. The once white paint, now a grayish-black, was covered in a layer of fuzz. This was the kind of dust a dreamy teenager could spend hours finger-writing her name and the name of the boy she loved in. She could draw hearts and "I love Jimmy 4-Eva's" in this dust. Or maybe it would be more like, "God help me to ever trust this whole Best Friends Forever concept again." Maybe a wiser, college graduate, would write in it something along the lines of, "You never really know a person until college orientation day." All I knew was I had a very strong urge to write, "Help!" in it as we climbed the creaky stairs to the second floor of the fraternity house. We were getting closer, with each rickety step, to the brooding pack of boy wolves on the roof. *Fuck!*

They say it takes the average college freshmen about a year to gain fifteen pounds and a month to get homesick. Ever the over achiever, I'd already reached homesick before even spending a night in my dormitory. But I was quite sure my XL giraffe-like frame would soon be down to a not-so-whopping 130 pounds. Homesick? That, I could understand. But gaining weight here, in a crack house lit with potential social situations that would set fear into any God-fearing recluse? *I. Think. Not.* Who was this brazen whore I was following?

When had she captured my best friend? And was it me who was supposed to rescue her? Those were the sort of questions I pondered as I followed her up beer-battered stairs, petrified.

If I thought things were bad on our mutual assent, I had no idea what true mortification was until about twenty minutes later on my solo decent down those same stairs. We'd been in the room of overanxious twenty-somethings less than a minute before the room owner introduced himself as "Spunk." Spunk and his frat boy friends had us surrounded like pigeons on a beach jonesing for an abandoned french fry before asking our names. I about spit out my wintergreen gum when I heard Amy's response. With a Hollywood red carpet flip of her longish fringe locks, she flamboyantly announced, "Hell-ooo. I'm Amee-li-ahhh!"

Amelia? What the hell? The thick, pretend-French accent my purely Irish friend used to enunciate her name was like something stolen from a bad, very bad, foreign B movie. I was half-shocked she hadn't found a way to attach subtitles to her tits, pushing out from behind her skimpy tank top. The pitch and thickness she'd used to announce herself screamed, "I'm the queen of England, look at my gorgeous sex appeal and feminine features, boys. I screw for fun…" Her voice was so unnatural I was sure I could see Spunk wince *for* her. But Amy, clearly having practiced her royal introduction at least two hundred times in the mirror without my knowledge, did not notice the chuckles coming from the older guys in the back of the room. I could practically hear them taking numbers. I hung my head. I hoped they wouldn't notice me.

Since when did we bring painted-on, white cut offs and thick Parisian accents to college? Had she packed these things like stowaway sidepiece trinkets saved for a sunny—"oh, my it's too warm in here"—day? Or was it merely an outfit for the next Frat Boys Gone Wild Freshman Gang Bang movie I hadn't been aware we were about to partake in producing? *Help! Get me out of here!*

We were unexpectedly saved by Paul, who'd arrived with one Budweiser in each hand. His cheeks were the color of cranberries. I'm not sure if it was from the early afternoon buzz or the pure mortification that now colored my own scarlet cheeks.

"Yah, um, she's my sister. And that's her friend," he said, pointing to me.

"Hi sis and friend," an obviously older student named Travis, who Amy would eventually screw and do lines of cocaine with, snorted. He was a shark on live bait. Swirling, he'd already assessed this French wannabe as a sure screw and the friend as an inconvenient carry on. He'd assessed correctly. I took the beer Paul offered, sipping at it while taking a mental inventory of the exact number of pieces of wintergreen gum left in the back pocket of my jeans—three. *Maybe Mom and Mrs. D won't be able to smell the beer on my breath when we get back...If we get back.*

"Hi! I'm Lisa," I said to Travis, extending my hand. A few of the brothers let out grunts. I kept my eyes on the beer-stained carpet, sinking against the poster-wallpapered sheetrock.

"Well, hello, Lisa," the token fat guy offered from the back corner of the room. Thankful for his acknowledgement, but hyper-aware that silent ownership tags were already being placed on us, I sighed gratefully. *At least he's tall. Yes, he's a cross between Belushi on "Animal House" and a hairy gorilla, but he's tall. All prehistoric Apes are tall.* Tall was, after all, a giraffe girl's number one requirement in a potential boyfriend. Was I even seriously considering this?

Amy had already downed her first beer and was more than happy to relieve me of mine before I was able to make my exit excuse. I didn't have to think very hard. The vultures were already hanging on Frenchie's every word and the silent promises she offered of—at the very least—a hand job.

"Nice to meet you guys, we sorta have to go. We just came by for a sec to see Paul," I fumbled. Paul looked up at me hopefully. I don't think a single other set of ears in the room heard me.

I tried nudging her.

"Ames?"

She shot me a look of "are-you-fucking-serious, home girl? I'm here to stay" and I knew better than to argue with it. I shrugged, quickly making my way out of there, but not before nearly poking my eye out with the antler of a stuffed buck at the base of the stairs. *Why hadn't I noticed this before?* The buck stared at me, boasting his offering of about forty pairs of women's panties and bras—hanging from his antlers. The lingerie came in a cheerful rainbow of sizes, fabrics, and styles. Apparently, my best friend was not the first freshman transplant around this joint. I literally ran out the door, nodding a goodbye to the underwear-rack-dead-buck and never more thankful for fresh air. I was numb to the guys laughing on the roof as I ran across the street and back toward campus.

Looking back, I'm not sure why I ever expected college for Amy to be anything but a seven-year drunken stupor, leading to an eventual drama or pottery degree. But I decided, at that moment, to accept my fate for what it was. And I did. I had to. She was, after all, all I had. Correction: I had her and the explanation I'd now have to come up with about the missing French coed, Amee-li-ahhh, formerly known as Amy, for the moms.

***

Amy, it turns out, was good practice for me. Ten years later, I was in exactly the same boat. I found myself again covering for, relying on, and worrying about another lover of the party and all things alcohol. This time, however, I had a lot more riding on it than back in 1992. Daisy dukes, strange guys in my doom room, and lost keys seemed like nothing compared to days missed on the job and the looming threats of quitting all the work Jeff had put into his degree; all because of alcohol.

December 23, 2001
Dear Mr. J,
The good news is that he's not going to drink to-morrow night at Mom's for Christmas Eve. Should that even be good news? I wonder how many

*women are worrying about this at this very mo-
ment. I wonder how many other people are watching their husbands count out thirteen beers this
very second.*

*He's so careful about it, the way he puts them in
the fridge. He makes sure all the tabs on the tops
of the cans face the same direction. I don't think
he's even aware that he does it. He told me he
wanted to die again today. He was sober when he
said it. Yet, he still says it's not "manly" to go talk
to a therapist. He has no idea how it makes me feel
to hear him talk like that. I wonder if he regrets
marrying me. I wonder if it's that I'm not a good
enough wife. I know I am a good mother. But maybe I'm doing something wrong? Maybe there is a
way to stop this?*

*I miss Amy. She'd know what to do. Then again,
she'd tell me it was no big deal. Amy could quit
anything. She quit smoking cold turkey and didn't
even get bitchy. Who does that? She's not talking to
me. She called me a few months back and asked
me to be in her wedding. I was overjoyed. I wanted
to do it so bad. But we didn't have the money for a
bridesmaid dress and the shower. Nate had a doctor's appointment that was more important. I
called her mother and asked if I could have a few
weeks to come up with the money. For some reason, that caused a huge brawl. Now she's not even
speaking to me. I have no idea who I can talk to
about this.*

*I am looking forward to tomorrow night. I know
we will have fun. Jeff will be on his best behavior.
He doesn't want anyone to know he drinks. I don't*

want them to know either. I just want a nice, normal Christmas. I want to pretend this isn't happening. And know what? That's exactly what I'm going to do. At least for one day. Ha! One day at a time. But for how many more days?

***

Self-Diagnosis: Enabler: Hardcore.

88 Bottles: Bell Bottoms & Loyalties
"Who were they to judge?"

Jeff was not initially "good enough" for my family. My mother so much as said that to me the night I brought him home with a shiny engagement ring to meet them—not something I would recommend. He grew up as a military brat. His family hopped from place to place, following his emotionally absent father's job around the country. His family finally settled in Rhode Island, where his father was making $11 an hour and Farmer Charming owned exactly two pairs of jeans. One pair was bell-bottoms. Ritzy Newport is a scary place for a boy with two pairs of pants and unusually greasy hair. He spent the next ten years of his life trying to fit in with the rich kids while I—four years younger and a hundred miles away—tried to push off teasing from the popular ones.

My mother, in particular, wasn't all that impressed by the cute cowboy promising her only little girl the world. And, it was true, promises only go so far when you are starving and have too much pride to ask for help. That's how we started out. I can't say I'd feel any different if Ella brought home a Farmer Charming. At first, it was cute, the way we scrounged change from the couch cushions to come up with enough money for Chinese food. Jeff never liked Chinese. He did it for me. He did a lot for me back in those days. And I loved him for it all the more.

In many ways, Jeff proved my family wrong about him. He is a hard worker and a good provider. He loves his family very much. He is quiet and reserved with a sharp sense of humor. In short, for an alcoholic, he's quite functional and not totally "checked out" like people might expect.

Our wedding was in January 1997 in Our Lady of Fatima. This was the church I'd grown up going to every Sunday with my eager mother, reluctant siblings, and begrudging father. It had rust colored carpets straight out of the 70s and is likely one of the ugliest churches I've ever seen. Unlike the ornate Catholic churches most would expect of the faith, this one was plain. I was okay with that. In fact, I preferred its simple lines and modest stained glass windows.

I really didn't have much say about where my wedding would take place, when I'd be married, or anything to do with our wedding day. It did not likely occur to anyone that some of my worst childhood memories came by way of rowdy fights between my parents on the way to and from that church. My mother took care of most of the arrangements. It was simple, practical, but most of all fast.

"Do you realize how badly you've hurt your mother?" my Grampy—Mom's father—asked me the summer following our marriage. "She didn't want your wedding to be like that." It was the only time Grampy, a dry alcoholic himself, ever scolded me and it stung. As a parent, I could understand his need to stand up for his daughter. But, holding my precious newborn, I had a hard time understanding how my son—or the circumstances of his birth— could ever be a disappointment to anyone. I nodded in agreement anyway, looking out onto the lake and reminding myself I had the life I'd been dreaming of as a child.

I'd learned I was pregnant with JJ the previous August. True to my loves-to-live-in-denial form, I'd hidden this from my parents until finally writing them a letter on my old word processor on Dec. 4, 1996—another mistake I wouldn't recommend. The only thing that pushed me to even write the letter then was knowing I'd be seeing them in three weeks for Christmas and was sure they'd notice I'd put on weight. Had that timing been different, I might have let my lifelong ability of lying to myself be an excuse to put off sending out news of the pregnancy until after he was born. Fortunately, Santa Claus pushed me in the right direction.

Jeff and I were engaged well before I became pregnant. My plan, I wrote in that letter, was that we would wait until after the baby, due in April, was born to get married. But Mom would hear nothing of the sort. She immediately cancelled my May 25, 1997 dream wedding and changed it to the first available date in January.

The bridesmaid dresses, now narrowed to only one maid of honor for practicality's sake—a job reserved only for Amelia-Amy—would be ruby red. The hall we'd planned to hold our reception at, The Forest Inn, was more than happy to accommodate the date change—freeing up a prime time slot for another, not shotgun, bride in May. I didn't argue on any of this. Instead, I spent my nights working on a cross-stitch bib for JJ after making calls to my three intended bridesmaids to cancel their plans of being in my wedding at all.

***

Self-Diagnosis: Submissive personality type, avoids conflict and authority at all costs. Knows when there are bigger fish to fry.

87 Bottles: On Honor
"When would he realize that I had none?"

In favor of our rushed engagement or not, Dad stayed up that night of my wedding eve writing me a ten-page letter I still keep in the hope chest Jeff made me as a wedding gift. A staunch pro-lifer, Dad was quiet during the three-week wedding planning frenzy. I knew he was constantly reminding my mother that I could have made another decision and not kept their first grandchild. In that letter is more love and advice than a girl could ever ask for from a man I never knew quite how to relate to. He encouraged me to remember never to go to bed angry and not to try to change a man. I've pulled out that letter over the years, not so much for the advice within it, but for the love Dad put into writing it. It's handwritten in blue, scratchy ink. He even took the time to print little pink hearts along the borders of the computer paper he wrote it on. Or, maybe, and more realistically, Mom did it for him.

While not big on giving advice in this format, my parents were huge on sending messages. They made a few things very clear to us as children. Mom spent every waking moment of our childhoods drilling it into our heads that education is a number one priority. (And Jeff hadn't finished his degree by the time I'd met and married him.) She'd back her message up with strict bed times, firm groundings, and more than a few teachers' conferences—anything to keep us on track at school. Though I had to work for it, I picked right up on her cues and became an honor roll student who would go on to graduate from college with honors in three years' time.

For Dad, it was all about honor: A quality he told my mother Jeff had, for marrying the girl he'd knocked up. *Honorable Jeff, lucky Lisa-soon-to-be-Livingston. Gag. Why hasn't anyone ever seen that he's the lucky one here, too?* Once, as an alter server for our church, I was asked to serve at someone's wedding. A romantic, I was excited to be a part of this stranger couple's special day. At the end of the service the bride's father handed an envelope to the priest, an envelope to the organ lady, and an envelope to me. I stood on the edge of the ugly rust alter wide-eyed. I had no idea there was something in this for me.

In my envelope was twenty-five dollars. I shrieked inside. Twenty-five dollars is a lot of money to a twelve year old. I snatched off my vespers and walked, robot-on-crack-style to my parents' car. My parents were thrilled with my excitement at the contents of the envelope. "Not bad, hon! You made twenty-five bucks an hour," Dad exclaimed. "Not bad at all." That excitement, however, had the shelf life of expired cottage cheese.

No sooner had I stepped into the back seat of the chocolate brown Honda than I noticed the organ lady chasing me to the car. "She stole money from the church!" she was yelling, frantically trying to get my father's attention as he began to pull out.

Confusion engulfed me. I knew I had not stolen anything and was tempted to look around the parking lot to see if this crazed organ lady had mistaken me for some other alter server who must have had a death wish or something. Nope, she was after me. I was sure of it as she banged on my father's driver side window.

Dad rolled down the window and asked the woman what she was talking about. He was out of the car in less than twenty seconds, telling me to do the same. He walked with me, hand in hand, back to the church. My fingers clutched his firm palm as he asked me, once, "Did you steal that money?" I burst into tears at the thought of it. "No!"

"Fair enough. I didn't think so."

Dad marched with all the conviction of a drum major in a world-class marching band into that church. We cruised past the bride and groom, still standing on the edges of the church, hoping to get last minute pictures of light reflecting from the stain glass windows onto her snowy dress. He walked passed the alter, past the choir room, past the children's room—reserved for the less-than-well-behaved parishioners such as my four younger brothers. It wasn't long before I found myself behind the alter, in the backroom where priests get dressed and swap jokes with deacons. There, he spotted the priest who had performed the ceremony. Ironically enough, he was just finished opening his very own envelope and seemed to be quite pleased at his "take" as well.

"That *bitch* is accusing *my* daughter of stealing money from the church," Dad said, slapping my envelope down on the cherry kneeler next to the priest. I don't know who was more shocked—me or the priest. First off, my father is the most religious person I know. For him to swear in a church, let alone in the back of the church, on the alter, was pretty much about as expected as the sun crashing into the earth full speed at 12:38 on a Tuesday afternoon. It just doesn't happen. But it was happening, right before my eyes.

"Slow down, Sir. Who? Who is saying what?" the startled priest asked.

"That *bitch*, what's her name? Jenny Blanchard's mom? Her. She's saying Lisa *stole* this envelope from the church," he stammered.

"There must be some confusion."

"You're damn right there's some confusion! My daughter doesn't *steal*! My daughter has *honor*. I taught her to have honor and I won't let anyone, especially not that horrible woman who can't even play the organ or hold a note, hurt her honor!"

It was less than twenty minutes before the priest and others, drawn in to solve the mystery of some missing envelope that was apparently intended for a choir member, realized that a missing check was actually stuck to the back of the organ lady's envelope.

"I told you my daughter has honor. Don't you *ever* question her integrity again," Dad barked after the mystery was solved. "Come on, hon. Let's go."

With that, Dad dragged me back to the car and spent, oh, a week or more repeating the same story over and over again to me, my mother, my brothers, and pretty much anyone willing to listen. "My daughter has honor and there is no one who is ever going to tarnish that," he'd say, like a scuffed New Kids on the Block record of the early 90s. *I wonder what he'd think of my summer camp lies?*

***

Maybe we *do* marry our fathers. Jeff has major issues when it comes to honor and Ella too. She couldn't have been more than five when he began plotting how he'd approach the first boy who decided to show up at the house to take her on a date.

"They are going to treat her with respect, Lisa. I'll go to jail for that kid, Lisa. You can laugh all you want, but I'm not having some asshole come in here and think he's going to fuck with my daughter," he'd say.

I'd respond, "She's five, honey. Chill out. It's going to be okay. You're going to be okay. I'm sure she'll only pick very respectful, very honorable boys, hon."

He'd turn to the boys, uninterested in arguing with me. "And you two clowns better treat girls with respect, got it? There's no hitting girls. Girls need to be treated with respect. You don't see me hitting your mother, do you?"

The poor boys. They were around eight and ten when those talks started. They haven't stopped.

It makes me laugh, now, knowing that things really don't work the same these days as he anticipates they will. I can't wait to see how he reacts to Ella being expected to meet a boy in a public place after "finding" each other on a phone app like Tinder. It's going to be hysterical, really. Let's just say that Jeff has not progressed with the times. He still carries around a candy bar texting phone and finds zero use for a smartphone. He's going to be in for a rude awakening when he learns what social media and the dating world is all about now. Luckily, we have a few years. I hope.

***

Self-Diagnosis: Daddy issues.

86 Bottles: Oh Boy(s)!
"Be practical, Lisa."

Pregnancy—even my first surprise pregnancy with JJ—was a delight. When I wasn't fearing my parents were going to kill me, I pulled out the dusty car ride fantasies of the family Jeff and I were going to create together. My Farmer Charming now had a face. He had strong hands and a big heart. I knew everything was going to be okay. In our engagement picture, taken in November of 1996, I wore a modest marquee diamond. I also had a sly grin on my face, my hands cupping my tiny stomach. I was holding and hiding my very own little secret—one I somehow knew would be one of the best decisions of my life. I was right. He was.

Jeff responded well to my being pregnant. We quit our Friday night bar dates and spent our free time making plans. We had long conversations about everything from how we would pay for college to who would be responsible for the bulk of the discipline and who would be on diaper duty. Typically, he hoped for a boy. Upon hearing this, I guilt-tripped him into how wonderful it would be to have a "daddy's little girl" around the house too. I said, "I'm so *sick* of boy this and boy that! Girls are great too. There's nothing wrong with a little girl." Less typically, he stared at me like he didn't recognize me. "You *know* I'm not like that, hon. I want a boy first so he can *protect* his little sister.

Geez, hon. *Chill out.*" He became set on that idea after the doctors told us we were, indeed, having a girl. We painted the nursery in our ghetto $500 per month apartment a bright pink and drew Care Bear designs all over the walls. We folded and refolded pink clothing in anticipation of her arrival. Jeff picked out a special cheerleader outfit for our daughter to wear home from the hospital.

Two days before my due date, my mother-in-law, Betty, Jeff, and I decided to kill time by going across state lines to Foxwoods Casino in Connecticut to play bingo. Betty, a registered midwife, said walking around the large casino might help bring on labor. I often joke that while I didn't win any money at the casino, I went home with the biggest prize that day. Sure enough, labor began, and nearly thirty hours and a very frantic ride back across state lines later, my blue-bundled "another-surprise" was born at 4:43 in the afternoon. *It's a what?*

Little Jeffrey weighed in at 7 lbs. and 3 oz. I will never forget holding him for the first time. The smell of him was something so sweet. His nose was wrinkled up like the Cabbage Patch kids Donna and I had once played with. His tiny hands were hardly big enough to curl around my thumb. On his head was a large patch of soft yellow curls. The surprise of having a boy definitely set us scrambling. Thankfully, Betty was able to return most of our pink clothes and exchange them for blue. Breast feeding, changing, and caring for our newborn seemed to make everything feel right. I no longer cared if my mother was angry with me for the timing of the pregnancy. She'd get over it. I didn't care that Jeffrey would go home to a Pepto pink nursery. He'd get over it too.

"Do you think he's going to grow up gay because of this?" Jeff asked.

"For starters, babies are colorblind, you dork! But more important, would we love him any less? Who cares if he grows up to be an alien. He's ours," I retorted, hugging JJ to my chest and growling at his father.

Jeff shrugged. "I guess not."

"We will fix it before he knows any different," I said.

Four months after having little Jeffrey— nicknamed "JJ" by his aunt—Jeff and I moved to be closer, a thirty minute ride, to my family. We lived in a garden apartment. Garden apartment is code for dark and dingy basement apartment. This particular dungeon was, however, in a nice complex owned by my mother's neighbors. Here, we spent some of the most happy years of our marriage.

Jeff—still unsure of what he wanted to do for his career but an avid animal lover—worked as a veterinary technician and part time carpenter and I freelanced for a local newspaper. I spent most days home with JJ and met Mom with JJ every Thursday for lunch. Those days with Mom and JJ were special. Still parenting my younger brothers, Jack and Josh, she made time to come out to spend time with her only grandchild. Long forgiven was the resentment about my getting pregnant out of wedlock. JJ stole her heart, just as he had mine. All was better now. It was a joy to watch her with him. I tried my best to learn from her, the way she handled him and what to and not to fret about. But I wanted to make my own rules. I also enjoyed my alone time with JJ. We especially loved our ritual of taking morning baths together. He was so comfortable with bath time that he was able fall asleep on my island stomach, bulging from the water and never quite flat again.

Life was simple. Our days were quiet: I had not discovered the Internet, though it was around. The archaic computer I did have was used only for my writing assignments. We didn't own cell phones and we shared a car—a mud brown Dodge Shadow. Our rent was $550 per month, including most utilities.

With things going well for our new happy family, I was anxious to give JJ a brother or sister. I asked Jeff for another baby and he reluctantly agreed. His primary concern was the financial strain of paying for formula and diapers. However, he was easily persuaded when I reminded him of our mutual dreams for a big family. I lost my first baby at nine weeks in August of 1998. I lost a second baby in November of 1998. I was devastated. Neither baby had a heartbeat and no one could tell me why this was happening. We'd decided to stop trying for a while when I discovered I was already pregnant and due in October, 1999.

With a new baby on the way, Jeff was concerned about finishing his education and beginning his career. He'd been unable to finish his bachelor's degree in environmental science when we first met because of the strains of marriage and parenthood. He enrolled in a new program in Massachusetts. "I need to be able to move up to support these kids," he reasoned. I agreed. If there was a point I could go back to and change, it was in agreeing that he should return to school full time with two kids under age three and still in diapers. It was just too much all at once. But you know what they say about hindsight...

Hindsight was something I had zero time for when I learned I was having another baby boy in July of 1999. I was glad JJ would have a brother—a built in best friend—to grow up with. However, I was secretly disappointed that this second child was not a girl. I knew better than to be fussy, though, after my bouts with miscarriage. I sincerely did believe the old "as long as the baby is healthy" mantra. To that end, I drove to a hundred miles every week to see a high-risk gynecologist. I made him reassure me, at least a half dozen times, that I was carrying a boy "for sure".

I still have an ultrasound photo of Nathan Eric with his penis circled in black marker. Nathan was born at 7:51 p.m. on October 2, 1999. He weighed in at a tiny 5 lbs. and 13 oz. I felt particularly blessed to hold this little miracle in my arms. He was a natural breast feeder and loved to snuggle. As an infant, he was an angel. The only time he would fuss, literally, was between the hours of 5 p.m. to 11 p.m. He had the most adorable, gummy smile. I took great delight in dressing him up as a pea pod that first Halloween. Life seemed perfect. And, in many ways, it was. I didn't need the farmhouse, the cows, or even the New York country-side. Everything I ever wanted was crammed into that tiny apartment, which we'd somehow managed to make feel like home. The only thing left was a little girl, Ella, who would come only two years later—*surprise again!*—by cesarean section and a whole lot of prayers to make our family complete.

***

Self-Diagnosis: Denial, stage one.

85 Bottles: Yellow Dollhouses
"The little things."

Mom bought countless popsicles the year I was in kindergarten. I am not talking about an ordinary amount of popsicles. I'm talking about boxes and boxes of them. She would hand them out to my friends and I like candy on Halloween with one condition: We had to save the sticks. She pushed these treats on us like a soldier on a mission. We never asked why. We did just as she asked and piled the sticks up on the kitchen counter, red lipped, and content.

The popsicles weren't the only quirky thing about Mom that summer. She asked strange questions like, "If you could paint our house any color, what color would it be?" and "When you grow up, what color will your house be?" I answered, "Yellow. Like Heather Thompson's." Yellow seemed like a fine color to me. Yellow was happy and the color of the sun. I didn't put much thought into it. The question seemed farfetched but I had better things to do like catching that salamander wedged under the rock wall in our woods than think about it.

A few weeks later, it was career day at school. When asked what my father did for a living, I responded, "He works in the basement." My teacher looked at me oddly, shrugged, and moved on. As far as I knew, that was true. My mother handed out popsicles and my dad spent every waking moment in the basement. At age five I had no way of articulating Dad's day job was working in engineering military defense systems.

That Christmas I was presented with an enormous gift. It was enormous both in physical size and in spirit. It was a handmade wooden dollhouse. The floors of the miniature house were hardwood made from mocha stained wooden popsicle sticks. Above the front door was a plaque that read, "Established, 1979." It was perfect. A few of the sticks in the hardwood gently hinted of the stains of the reds and oranges from where my friends and I had sucked. It was a sunny yellow. My father, it seemed, had spent all that time in the basement working on this project for me. And my mother, it turned out, was not so crazy after all.

I adored that dollhouse. I'd spend hours on end cramming plastic furniture into different corners of it and pretending I was living there. In the dollhouse, I was in charge. I was the mom and the kids did what I told them to do, not the other way around. In the dollhouse, I was loved by a man, one man, the man of my dreams. My favorite childhood toy, I took good care of the dollhouse and brought it with me into my adult life. It was one of the only toys that survived my childhood clumsiness and my rowdy brothers.

More than twenty years later, my husband started disappearing. By this time, we were living in a rented old Victorian home in Vermont. It was 2002 and I was beginning to feel like a pregnant gypsy. We often joked that we'd lived in just about every state in New England and would soon have to move south to explore that part of the country. This house was barnyard red; not unlike his temper by then. He was drinking constantly and often went missing into the barn beside our rented home. I dismissed his absences for trying to make an effort not to drink around me and our boys. *What the hell is wrong with him? Why can't he just stop? Will he always be this way? Is it school? Is it me? Why is he doing this to us?* These were the questions I didn't dare speak aloud.

On my 29th birthday, only days before our daughter was born, I was overwhelmed when he presented the other half of the yellow dollhouse to me. He'd completely recreated my original doll-house, adding a garage where the white balcony porch stood on the first. When matched up, the two houses closed into the perfect block. Atop the door, a plaque read "Established, 2002." With his absences now accounted for, I could barely live with the guilt of assuming the worst. He wasn't drinking. He was making a home—literally and figuratively—for me. For all of us.

***

Years later, it's late autumn when Jeff returns from work. His tie is twisted and crooked but his usual post-work scowl is missing. His eyes are bright as he walks in the house.

"Hon, did you ever notice that maple tree in the front yard?"

I look up from the oven, where I've just pulled out a pan of fried chicken and tater tots. The microwave is beeping, letting me know the frozen peas and carrots are ready. Steam is fogging my glasses and I squint to get a better look at him.

"No, I hadn't noticed. Why?"

"Come see it! "

I clench my fingers in my pockets. The kids have homework to do, including a huge state project for JJ that's due in only a few days. The animals haven't been fed. There are four loads of laundry that need folding sitting in the middle of the couch calling out for me. I don't want to go out and analyze trees in the yard.

"Let me grab my shoes," I say, smiling. *Love is an action, Lisa.*

I follow my husband to the front yard of our first home, which would turn out to be our 'forever home'. He holds smaller trees and branches back so I don't trip over them as I follow about ten steps behind him. He's moving quickly, like a kid on Christmas running to fetch his presents. After about a hundred feet, we come to the maple. I gasp.

"Wow. It's gorgeous! How have we never seen it before?"

The tree is grand with arms that span a large wooded section of the front yard. Its top branches are so long they form a graceful arch over the road in front of the house. Her fiery leaves are mostly gone but form a beautiful quilt at her roots, as if keeping her warm for the winter. Her strong, thick trunk shines in the quickly fading light and mirrors the twinkle in his eyes. He doesn't have to tell me what he's thinking.

"It would be beautiful!" I exclaim, completely forgetting about the laundry and homework.

Three weekends later, Jeff has single handedly cleared the wooded area of the front yard. He's called for loam and the maple tree stands proud and impossible not to notice. It's an unseasonably warm November afternoon and Jeff hangs a tire swing on her proud shoulders while JJ and I carve a tattoo in the shape of a heart on her stomach. In the heart, we carve the initial 'L' for our last name. The boys spend hours taking turns being pushed by Jeff while I take pictures and wish the moment would freeze itself in time. I have my maple tree, complete with the swing. Ella giggles as Nathan takes a turn at pushing her. Again, I feel guilty for giving him shit about drinking a few beers every now and then to unwind. We haven't fought in months. *I'm an asshole.*

***

Self-Diagnosis: Disloyal Judas. (Co-dependent style.)

84 Bottles: Real Life Dollhouse
"I am almost able to forget about
our disease."

These days, our forever house is not yellow. Though, coincidently enough, Jeff has also always dreamed of living in a yellow house with white trim. Instead, it is a flat almond with periwinkle shutters. We bought the home in 2004—not long after he built me the mini, dollhouse version. A modest but cozy modular ranch, it was a place to call our own; tucked neatly into the hills of Vermont.

We live in an old mill town. Established in 1762 at the base of a well-loved mountain, it boasts exactly one Minute Mart, one mechanic, three protestant churches, and one Catholic church which was closed in 2006 when the parish experienced a sharp decline in parishioners because of bad publicity about priests' activities with altar boys. Our town also has a pond for swimming, an elementary school, and an abandoned textile mill. That's it, folks.

The average family income for a family of four is not far above the poverty level and average education is high school. Children of children of children were taught by the same teachers as their parents and often live with, or nearby, grandparents. Many of the baby boomers in town worked in the mills and have not worked since the mill shut its doors in 2002. But despite the financial strains, people here look out for one another. The quintessential New England town, it offers a sense of community where everyone knows everyone's names, brand of cigarettes, and Old Home Day is something everyone looks forward to. People still run tabs at the Common Minute Mart for gas, rubbers, hot dog buns, and wine coolers. Families of all ages come out once a month to support the local senior center during breakfasts where everyone eats buffet style for under $5 per person.

Despite our skeletons, Jeff, the boys, Ella and I have managed to create too many good memories to count in this home. There is no father I know who spends more time playing with his children than Jeff does with ours. On days like today, when JJ comes home from college for Columbus Day Weekend, I love watching the four of them kick around a soccer ball and laugh as he blows past them on the makeshift field in our backyard. I laugh when the kids gang up on him, hoping that maybe this one time they will be able to beat Dad at his own game. (They rarely do.)

Later, after JJ's gone off with his hometown girlfriend and Nathan's out with friends, I am distracted from my writing. I look out the window as Jeff pushes Ella on the tire swing, watching her reach higher and higher into the gray, chilly sky. I see endless possibilities in their movements and togetherness. I'm not afraid for her future or ours.

On these sober days, Jeff makes a huge effort to spend time with me. It is the moments like these that are drops of water in the desert that has often become our marriage. His love hydrates me when we go to shops or flea markets together. Other times, we rent movies and watch them as a family. I never fail to gulp on these moments where I am married to the same man I fell in love with. He is my best friend. My children are happy and laughing. There's even a pet cow in our backyard. If you breathe deep, you can smell the faint odor of potential that I fantasized about as a kid. In these moments, I am almost able to forget about our disease. I am able to taste the lemon sugar sweetness of my childhood dreams and look at him most sympathetically, realizing we are not so different. We both love and bleed the same—deeply. Him, just deeper than me.

***

Self-Diagnosis: (Still) a hopeless romantic.

83 Bottles: Fetch My Soup!
"I'll never marry a sexist!"

As a kid, I looked up to Mom for her ability to always cheer me on, regardless of how embarrassing it must have been for her to be the mother of the worst dancer, last to finish every race, worst athlete, etc. I often wondered why she hadn't made more of an effort to cheer for herself. The natural feminist in me was always irritated that she spent more time doing dishes, laundry, and grocery shopping than anything else. Her weekly trips to the dry cleaners with my father's suits particularly annoyed me. *Doesn't she have anything better to do? She's certainly smart enough*, I'd ask myself, but never her. I spent the better part of my childhood watching her—the way she took care of her family and home. She moved like a weed in the wind; strong, natural, and unyielding. I admired it but feared it. And for good reason.

Mom talked often about having been abused at the hands of her alcoholic father, Grampy. Sometimes, I wondered how this had affected her. I'd ask, *Is this why she isn't more outspoken about her own career goals and aspirations? Or is she just that dedicated to the family? Will I be this way with my own family? Should I? Is this love or madness?* These were big questions for a nine-year-old. They were questions I can't answer now, even in my forties. But I never stopped asking them. I still wonder, even now that everything's changed.

Mom said Grampy hit her so hard sometimes when he drank that she urinated in her clothes to get him to stop. I guess, by the contexts she'd tell me this story in, I was supposed to feel thankful I wasn't punished so severely for offenses like hiding spelling tests under my bed. In some ways, I was thankful. I knew, just from her stories, that it could have been much worse. "Alcoholism," she warned, "is a horrible, horrible thing." I promised myself never to marry an alcoholic. Later, I told myself Jeff couldn't really be *that bad*. He never hit anyone.

Things weren't so rosy on my father's side either. About once a month, we'd get a visit from my father's parents. Grandpa and Grandma had a unique relationship. He ignored her. And the more he did, the more she persisted with him, anxious for any—even negative—attention. Of course, the more she did this, the more he ignored her. Their mean spirited repartee with one another made me uneasy and constantly searching for an excuse to play in my room while they visited with my folks.

Before my grandparents arrived, Mom brewed up a delicious batch of corn chowder or sausage and peppers. Her soup made the house smell like a friendly pub and I took great joy in spicing it up with salt and pepper as I pathologically checked on her progress. Frantically, we'd clean, the bitter taste of Windex mixing in the stale air, to make sure things were perfect for the visit. My four brothers were never asked to help. Boys didn't do things like that. Boys weren't made for kitchens. "It's good bonding time, Lisa," Mom would say, leaving me screaming on the inside. Saving the kitchen floors for last, Mom was sure to cut up cheese and pepperoni or make shrimp cocktail for stow-away snacks for their impending tag-team Canasta games. I'd watch her play the Stepford game, then, I'd plot my escape.

When Grandma, with her purple nose—from poor circulation, according to doctors and an evil spell placed on her as a child by a witch, according to her—would peek her head in the door, I smiled. But when Grandpa followed behind, my throat would get dry and something inside of me would grow quiet and angry. I knew what Grandpa would do before he did it. He'd order me to get him a bowl of soup and pour him a soda—7Up or Sprite. He would never ask any of my brothers, who may have been closer by or not in the middle of some-thing. He was insistent that Mom relax and I, being the only other female hostess in the house, should dedicate my night to serving him. I felt like some-one should be giving this man a bell and forcing me to chew on grass in the backyard while I waited for his next command. I promised myself I'd never marry a sexist either. That one, I followed through on. And I'm glad.

A person can see some things coming easier than others. Or, maybe, you chose to ignore certain things. While Jeff drinks more than anyone I've ever met, he's the last person on earth I'd call sex-ist. *Does that make it a fair trade off? One out of two ain't bad?* I'd ask myself this and still do.

***

Self-Diagnosis: Angry feminist whose future sons would be forced to know how to 1. Do laundry, 2. Work a kitchen, and 3. Scrub floors. Also, determined to marry a man who knows how to and does all of the above, regularly. Without being asked. (End rant, for now.)

82 Bottles: Coffee Tables & Spit "Where is the man who once defended my honor?"

While hindsight is twenty-twenty, there are moments that are impossible to ignore *as* they occur. One of these things happened to hit me—literally—one night after a horrible fight and ten beers killed off by my non-sexist, yet very alcoholic husband.

Feeling brave, I approached Jeff while he hand-washed dishes. He had a beer in one hand and the other hung at his side. He was leaning his full body weight on the counter, which was also lined with seven empties. It was then—maybe because it was early on in his drinking or maybe because I was having a bout of "I am woman, hear me roar"—that I decided to ask him to stop drinking. Regardless, I don't remember putting any thought into my timing; something not typical of me.

"We've got to talk about this, hon," I said, closing in on him at the kitchen sink. My hips were squared off and I gripped the edge of the sink with my left hand, physically boxing him in.

He wobbled, shifting his weight from one foot to the other. I was glad the boys were safely upstairs, playing on their Nintendo system in the playroom. I'd put Ella down hours ago.

"What's there to talk about?" he retorted. His scowl told me he was defensive. "I'm a grown fucking man! I can do what I want to do in my own house. What the fuck?"

Jeff's always had a way with cursing. There's no word too strong for him. But when he's drinking, he tends to use fuck as not only a verb, but an adjective, a noun, and even a pronoun—"Fucker thinks she's going to tell me what to do. Fuck that." I knew, from word choice alone, his buzz was even higher than I'd anticipated. I immediately went into playing offense. Opposing teams in a championship game, we were at a face off. We were going into overtime. One of us would walk out a winner. The other would be defeated.

"It's not "what the fuck". It's *not* "what the fuck"! It's fucking *serious*. It's not funny anymore! It's not *cute* and it's not *okay*! You have *kids*. You have a wife. You are a *grown* man! Why can't you *act* like one?"

"Fucking grown man? You think I'm not a grown fucking man? What do you make, $12 an hour at that shitty reporting job of yours? It's all on me. Don't you get that? It's all on me! I put this fucking roof over you guys' heads! I go to work every day. I work two jobs. What the fuck do you want from me?"

I snapped. I reached across him and grabbed a full can of beer from the counter. He'd just cracked it open, taken a sip, and put it back down. I took it and dumped it down the sink.

"I want you to *stop*! I want you to pick! It's us or beer. You pick!" I lunged at him, screaming in his face in a way I'd never done before.

I was no more than an inch from his face, ranting at him to "grow up" when he took another sip of a new beer and spit it directly in my face.

"*Pick?* Pick, cunt? You got it. I pick *beer*."

He grabbed two more bottles and left the room as I stood in front of the sink, stunned, beer dripping from my glasses and cheeks. I stayed there for an hour, eventually sliding down to the kitchen floor, where the beer on my face mixed with my tears. I shook, staring down at hands that had their own agenda. *Thank God the kids didn't hear that. This has got to stop.*

Something about having him spit beer in my face or maybe the word he'd called me made me angrier than I'd ever been. Kids who'd made fun of me in high school, the guy who raped me in college, the sneers and whispers of kids who thought they were better than me, my grandfather's demands that I serve him—all of those things came back. *Fuck this! I'm fucking done. I'm not a fucking victim.*

I jumped from the floor, wiped off my face, and went to find Farmer Asshole. He was upstairs in our bedroom, reading—of all things—a book on religion. *Did you get to the part about not being an asshole? What about the parts on treating your family right?*

"You're not going to just spit beer at me and think that's okay, you prick!" I screamed at him, knocking the book out of his hand. I knew I was pushing him. A big part of me wanted him to hit me. And at some point, I told him to. "Hit me, pussy! Show me how much of a *man* you really are!" I knew, if he hit me, I'd have an excuse to leave and never look back: *Guilt, loyalty, vows, be gone.* The neighbors, and what they might think? Irrelevant. If only he would hit me physically. The rest felt like it didn't count. It was never quite close enough, or so I thought. But Jeff wasn't—and never could be—physically abusive and I knew it. I resented him for that. I wanted out. I wanted him to buy me that free ticket out so I could be free without blame.

We fought the rest of the night like mortal enemies. He picked up the coffee table and threw it at me. It caught me on the shoulder, leaving a bruise. But the bruise was nowhere as big as the one on my ego when I left the house that night with the kids to call my parents for help. *I'm not lying for that prick anymore. I need someone to help me. To help us. The kids deserve better than this.*

With tears fogging up my glasses, I drove our half-sleeping children to a parking lot about a mile from the house. By then, Jeff was passed out and had no idea we'd even left. I'd given up fighting with him. He wasn't going to hit me—at least not with his fists—and I wasn't going to get him to stop drinking. I had admitted my defeat—for now—and was more interested in winning the war than the battle. I dialed my parents' number.

Sobbing, I recounted parts of the story to Mom.

"I can't understand you, hon. Slow down," she said, telling my father to pick up the phone on the other line. Her voice carried the patience it had for Grandpa when asking for a third bowl of soup from the stove only three feet away from him.

"Did he hit you?" Dad asked.

"No. He didn't hit me, but he threw a fucking coffee table at my head! It hit my shoulder."

"Was he aiming to hit you?"

"I don't think so, Dad. I think he was throwing it out of frustration and I sort of walked into it." *Why does him asking that piss me off so bad?*

"Fights do happen, hon," Dad said. *Where the fuck is the guy who defended me at the church when I didn't steal? Isn't it a father's job to protect his only daughter?*

My jaw dropped. I didn't know what to say. How was it possible that my father was so calm about what seemed so serious to me? I had flashbacks to the fights I'd seen my parents have pretty much every Sunday of my entire childhood. Once, my mom had been so mad that she tried to jump out of the car while Dad was driving us to church—late for mass, again. Another time, she poured a full glass of ice water over his head. Countless times, even on Christmas once, my father had been so angry that he'd left the house barefoot to drive to his brother's house and spend the night there just to avoid confrontation. He'd never hit her either. And trust me, she'd begged for it in her own ways too. *Was it man code*, I wondered, *that it was okay to push the lines with your wife, as long as you didn't punch her square in the nose and break it?* I was beginning to hate all things men, including this code I didn't understand. *Why can't I be a lesbian?*

"You can come here if you want to, hon." Mom said.

"I know, Mom. But I can't drive right now. I'm too upset. I'm going to go to Jaymee's house." Jaymee was a good friend from work who lived in town and was single. She adored my kids and I knew she'd have no problem with us crashing there for the night.

I talked with my parents a little more. Overall, it calmed me down, but their advice was startling. To paraphrase, Dad basically told me the best thing to do was to go to church and say a novena. A novena is a week of dedicated prayer that you also write down. After a week, God answers this form of prayer. He told me to pray for Jeff to be happier and healthier and for things to work out in our marriage. *Excellent. Jesus saves! I'll get right on that, Dad. Only, I've been writing this prayer for years now in my journal and he—of course God is a man, why would a woman ever get to be the one in charge—hasn't seemed to care yet.*

Mom, on the other hand, told me about how if she was me, she'd be terrified. She'd want a "back up plan". She reminded me of a guy who'd had a crush on me in high school and told me he was currently single. He had taken a job as a coach at my old high school.

"You know, hon, Pete's been asking about you a lot lately. Every time he sees me, he asks me how you are doing," she said. I could hear the hopefulness in her midnight voice.

"Jesus, Mom! You're worse than Dad. He wants me to pray and make it go away and you want me to have an affair?"

"No! Not an *affair*. I'm just saying. If things don't work out with you and Jeff, there are other guys out there," she said. "Look at Aunt Martha! She's been married three times already! Things are different now! People do get divorced, you know." *Really, Mom? I wasn't aware of that. Thanks! That's exactly what I need. I need to think of another man right now.* But as much as I wanted to scream at her, take it all out on her, I also loved that she was right there, ready to cheerlead for me if I decided to dump Jeff and take up with the local former-fat-kid gone gym teacher. "Whatever makes you happy, hon," she'd said. *Why can't Jeff be that easy? If he truly cared about my happiness, none of this would be an issue at all.*

The prospects of intense prayer or a booty call with a former bully lineman turned repentant didn't seem like the best of options. In fact, going back to Farmer Drinks-A-Lot seemed better than either of those. So after I hung up with Mom, I drove home, put the kids to bed, and cried myself to sleep next to Nathan. Fortunately, he's a deep sleeper and was clueless. *Tomorrow is another day. He'll be sober and it'll all be okay.*

If you haven't figured it out yet, I am slow to learn sometimes. I see the good in people and hang on to it like a snow cone on a hot day. But after you've had a six-foot cherry coffee table come flying at you, you tend to see things for what they are pretty quickly. While Jeff was sober and apologetic the next morning, things didn't really look all that much better to me.

I didn't know what to do. I didn't know who I could call that might possibly give me better advice than I'd just received. I didn't know anything, really. Except that I wanted to escape. *Yes, I will change my name, change my story, change my life. I'll do it just like I did at summer camp. Instead of being Lisa-Wife-Of-Beer-Spitter, I'll become Lisa-Never-Got-Married-Free-Spirit with kids. I'll change the kids names too. JJ can be Ever-Take-A-Sip-Mom'll-Kill-Me and Nate will become Don't-Touch-The-Stuff. Ella? She'll be a lesbian and can keep her name. It's crap we woman are always the ones giving up our names. We'll live together in harmony, working on legislation for the reinstatement of prohibition. Of course, I'll raise them to be glorious feminists who'd never dare demand a woman bring them corn chowder. They'll prefer shining coffee tables with Murphy's Oil to throwing them. And, at the very least, they'll spit into sinks after brushing their teeth—but never in anger.*

***

Self-Diagnosis: Escapist with big, bullshit, plans.

81 Bottles: Playing Doctor
"Who was truly the sick one?"

Over the years, I've read as many books as I can find on the topic of alcoholism, particularly on being the wife of an alcoholic. There really aren't that many of them, unless you count self-help books. Personally, I find them preachy. When I want a sermon, I go to church. Regardless, I was desperate and determined to find out if I'd somehow predestined myself for this fate in picking my spouse. *Was it that I was an insecure child who grew into an insecure adult? I'd certainly done some silly things for attention and to feel loved before. How would this be any different?* I'd wonder.

At one point, I read something about how a woman's first experiences with boys or men often defines the choices they make down the road. This makes me think of an incident involving the all-important neighbor boys. It's a memory that embarrasses me now, as a mother of three, but it's one I think is important to share because it shows just how screwed up I was from a very early age.

***

1984

I take my time in selecting my underwear this morning. I know Jarod and Hayden will be expecting something cute. *What do boys even consider cute? Maybe I should wear the ones with the pink hearts? Or what about the ones with the tiny blue dots? Yes. These are the ones. Blue is Jarod's favorite color. I will wear these.*

I pull tiny pink shorts over the prized panties, giggling at my secret. I wonder how long it will take them to invite me behind the tree. I wonder what they will think when they see these special panties. They were so proud of me yesterday, just that I'd had the nerve to show them at all. And those yesterday panties were plain white cotton.

My heart races as I speed through a bowl of Applejacks and turn down Mom's famous pancakes. I need to get this day started, to get outside to a place where boys and big fat trees rule the world: To the place where I rule the world. My magic wand, my super power, is these prized panties. They make boys like me.

They were shy at first. Jarod wouldn't look me in the eye and Hayden's ears were the color of rubies. I didn't mind. It just meant they were thinking the same thing I was thinking. We stood in my front yard, going over things to do for the day.

"We could work on the fort," I offered, hoping to get them out toward the woods.

"No, I'm sick of the forts," Jarod said.

"Yeah, me too," Hayden agreed. "We wanna play inside, but our mom said no. She's cleaning."

"That's okay. I know we can find something to do out here. My mom won't let us go in either."

Jarod was watching the dirt collect on his white tennis shoes as he dug them into my parents' lawn. I wondered how long it would take him to look up at me. I had a good three inches on him, even though we were both nine.

"Well," he began, followed with the longest silence I'd ever heard. "We could, um, go check out that tree again."

Hayden grinned and my heart jumped. The butterflies came rushing back to my belly and it took everything I had in me not to scream a loud, "Yes!" or "Finally!"

I shrugged, "Okay. If that's what you want to do." I reached up and twirled my yellow, brittle hair between my thumb and pointer finger. "Let's go."

Their eyes were heavy on my butt as they followed me into the woods behind my parents' house. I tried to sway my hips the way I'd seen the skimpily clad Daisy Duke do it on "The Dukes of Hazzard," a show my parents allowed me to stay up for on Friday nights. They were watching me like Bo and Luke watched Daisy and I knew it. I walked very slowly to the now-famous 'Big Fat Tree' and they stayed a few steps behind me. I didn't look back at them.

When we got to the tree, it was seven-year-old Hayden who was the bravest.

"Show us!" he demanded.

I looked over to Jarod, whose eyes were stuck on the base of the tree stump as he tossed a pinecone back and forth, back and forth, between its roots.

"Show us!" Hayden repeated.

This time, Jarod looked up, nodding in agreement with his younger brother.

Carefully, cautiously, like it was the first time I'd ever done it, I lowered my pink shorts to my thighs. Their eyes got bigger. I tried not to laugh. My heart was beating so heavy now that I could see it drumming in the veins of my wrist. A breeze pushed against my naked thighs as I stood there, not sure what to do next. *Don't they know this is no different than a bathing suit? What idiots boys are,* I thought.

"I picked these out for you, Jarod. Blue is your favorite color. Do ya like em?" I tripped over the question, but still managed to get it out.

He nodded, this time faster. He moved forward to touch the elastic waistline. I sucked in a quick shot of air. I almost started coughing, not realizing I had been holding my breath to suck in my stomach. Instead, I laughed. Hayden took this as a sign that it was okay to touch and moved closer behind me. He ran his hand along my backside and gently swatted at it. I pushed his hand away. Jarod stepped back, but I was quick enough to pull his hand back in. This time, I pushed his hand down the front of my panties and was pleased with myself and him when he kept it there. He moved his hand there, for a few seconds, figuring out what was what, and finally laid his palm flat against my private parts. I felt a tingling I'd never felt before.

Hayden stepped back and watched as Jarod began to rub at my vagina with his fingers. He did this for a minute or two and quickly pulled his hand back, leaving me wanting more and a little startled. I searched his face, trying to figure out what he was thinking.

"We should go," he said. "If your parents catch us we're gonna get in trouble."

"But it's my turn, Jar! You said you guys would show me yours today." I have no idea what made me say this. I really didn't care about seeing anything of his. I had four brothers. Boys were no mystery to me. Looking back, I think this was about power. About evening the score. But at the time, my own demands confused me.

"We'll get in trouble!"

Hayden didn't seem to care. He pulled his denim cut offs over his thighs quickly and stood there in tight white underwear. He reached for my hand and put my fingers inside an opening in the front. His skin was warm and damp. He was breathing harder than usual and looking over at Jarod as if to say, "I got her to do it!" His grin spoke more words than he could possibly have said in that moment and I felt like the queen of the world. I tugged at him for a moment, not sure if I was doing this right, and smiled coyly at Jarod.

"Your turn."

He looked back at the tree roots. "Tomorrow. I swear! I don't wanna get caught! We've been out here awhile. I think someone's coming!"

I dropped my hand from Hayden's underpants and quickly pulled up my shorts. Panic ran through me as I looked around the woods and at the small opening to my parents' yard to see if he was right. But there was no one. I knew there wouldn't be, even before he said it. The only person who might have caught us was my brother Robbie. But Robbie wasn't a rat. He never told on anyone. He hated conflict more than I did.

The moment lost, we headed deeper into the woods to make a fort. Hayden was giving Jarod a dirty look and I wasn't sure what to think. I suspect, they didn't either. We didn't talk about it for the rest of the day. Hayden and Jarod went home for lunch and didn't come back like they usually did. They didn't come back until the next day.

It was Thursday and rainy out. I jumped up from the cross-stitch project Mom had me working on when I heard the doorbell ring. I searched my brain to make sure I had on good panties. *Yes, the pink ones,* I told myself, as I went to answer the door.

Jarod was standing there, alone. I was pleased. Something about him being less pushy than his brother made me like him best.

"Wanna come over? Mom said we can play inside."

"Yeah! Let me get my sweatshirt and tell my mom."

"Okay."

"Come in, silly, it's raining out!"

"Okay."

He stood in the front foyer, looking up at the large staircase that lead to my off-limits bedroom. There was a huge chandelier hanging from the cathedral ceiling. I ran to find my mother and after getting her permission to play at the Levin's house for the day, I skipped to the foyer to meet him.

"Let's go."

"Okay."

We walked to his house in silence. It didn't bother me. Jarod never said much. He didn't have to. His eyes were the color of limes and his smile made the butterflies come back to my belly. We'd been friends since we were four, but I was just noticing those eyes and that smile this summer. Maybe it was because he'd noticed my panties—me—first, I wasn't sure. Looking back, all I can see is Chuck—my cousin's friend—in that sleazy basement. It's amazing how patterns repeat themselves: Lisa wants and needs approval from men. At any cost. Repeat. Lisa stays with a drunk in the name of loyalty, but really, insecurity. Repeat.

Susan Levin had cookies waiting for us when we walked into the door.

"Wait! Stop! Take off your shoes," she squealed.

Moments later, we were plopped down in the basement, where Jarod and Hayden's much older step-brother slept, watching TV on the sofa. I was on my third chocolate chip cookie when Hayden announced that he had something to show me.

"Actually, this is Jarod's idea," he said. "But he didn't want you to get mad."

I looked at Jarod inquisitively, curious about what Hayden was referring to. Nothing was going to make me mad at Jarod. Didn't he know that? I wished Hayden would leave: Leave us alone.

"What is it?"

Hayden moved to the other end of the basement to his step-brother's bed. He lifted the red comforter and mattress on the right side and pulled out a tattered *Playboy*. He brought it to us, triumphantly.

"Check this out! These girls are like you," he announced.

My eyes were huge tan marbles—wobbly and unfocused—as I watched him flip from page to page. Women were spread, in all their naked glory, across the pages for anyone to see. *These* women didn't hide behind oversized maple trees. *These* women wore sparkly fuchsia cowgirl hats and tiny lace leotards to match their flirty smiles and pouts. I wanted a closer look: to understand what their magic was. I was tempted to grab the magazine from Hayden's hands but I didn't want Jarod to think I was weird. Instead, I let him flip through the pages and tried to seem unimpressed. I sighed and looked around. I ignored Hayden, as he pointed to his favorites. It didn't matter. Jarod wasn't looking anyway. He was looking at the floor.

"Do this!" Hayden finally commanded, spreading the open magazine to its centerfold across the makeshift milk crate coffee table. "Jar! Get up! She needs room!"

The glossy young centerfold was staring up from a sofa couch, naked from the waist up, playing with her panties. Her blue eyes were pleading for someone to call her beautiful, something I'm sure Hayden couldn't see. I couldn't miss it. Her breasts were swollen and capped off with cherry-sized nipples of the same color. Her freckled arms lay gracefully over her tight stomach, leading the way to her curious fingers and the slightest patch of ruby-colored pubic hair.

I began to cough. I'm not sure what made me cough. Maybe it was the air I'd sucked in so fast upon seeing this girl; so exposed and vulnerable, yet powerful all at once. Or maybe it was because I'd forgotten to breathe all together. Perhaps it was nerves? I wish I could say the cough was my way of rebelling—a hope at getting out of the situation: A moment of unprecedented self-worth. But the truth was, all I could think about was mimicking that fiery beauty queen's pose.

But I couldn't stop coughing. My throat betrayed me with ugly hawk noises for a good three minutes. Hayden gave me a dirty look, anxious to get on with the show. What he didn't understand was that I wasn't happy about it either. I was as anxious as he.

"Shut *up*!" Hayden plea-barked, as the door leading to the basement stairs creaked.

"You okay down there?" Susan called down the stairs.

Hayden jumped over the back of the couch, magazine in hand, as quick-thinking Jarod called up a, "Yeah, we're fine, Mom."

I continued to cough. Eventually, I coughed so hard that Susan sent me home for medicine with a phone call to my mother. I spent the rest of the day on my own couch, trying to figure out how the beauty queen had spread her legs that far apart while looking entirely casual about it and gorging myself on Mom's homemade chicken noodle soup. I was certain I was going to hell. *At least, now, I'll have something to tell the priest about at penance. I wonder if that girl does penance too.*

Jared and Hayden never did take that magazine out again. I assumed Susan found it and took it away from them, but never dared to bring it up. But I took it out every day. Many times a day, in fact—in my mind. I became obsessed with it. No longer did showing off my panties make my heart race. Instead, it was the idea of showing hundreds of strangers my private areas that made me get that rush. I wanted to be her. I wanted to show men and even women my beauty and to have them stare back at me in awe. I wanted to wear the tiny lace thongs and sexy cherry bras I'd seen in that precious three minutes of Hayden's page-flipping. To me, it meant power and control; two things I lacked all together.

I looked forward to going to bed at night so I could hide in my room and stare into my dresser mirror and practice pouty faces. I wanted to master the beauty queen's artful stare. I even volunteered to do laundry so I could steal my mother's DD bras and washcloths. I'd use the washcloths to fill the bras and secretly chastise her for not having something more lacy. *Who in the world would wear plain cotton when they could get something lace and black? She must not know any better. She must never have seen a magazine like that,* I told myself.

I spent so much time alone, fantasizing and praying to God for boobs and my first period that I almost forgot about Jarod and Hayden all together. They'd come over to see if I wanted to play over the past weeks, but I'd made up excuses to decline. I didn't have time to be showing them my silly cotton underwear. I had bigger plans. I needed to practice for the strangers who would one-day want a peek at my perfect smile and huge breasts.

It was a typical, boring summer day and I was mid-fantasy when my mother began shrieking at me from the base of the stairs.

"Get your ass down here, young lady!"

I snapped up from my oh-so-seductive Marilyn Monroe pose and scanned my brain for what I possibly could have done wrong. She couldn't have found my F reading test, I reasoned. That was tucked neatly under my mattress and school was out for summer anyway. It couldn't have been the dishes. I'd made sure to do them well so she'd leave me alone. I hadn't been mean to my brothers. I hadn't even seen them. *What is her problem now?*

I groaned, trudging toward the top of the stairs.

Mom was seething. Her full lips were pressed into tight lines. Her hazel eyes were shooting hate seeds at me faster than I'd ever seen. Blood rushed through my limbs and I could feel the red racing toward my neck and cheeks.

"What'd I do?"

"You know what you did! Your father is going to be furious! Furious! I can't even look at you!" she said. "That was Susan calling. Do you know what she told me?"

I gulped, praying it wasn't what I thought it was. *No, it couldn't be! That was weeks ago. And there's no way those two would have ratted me out. They did it too. It has to be something else! Please, God. Let it be something else.*

"She told me she found Hayden with a dirty magazine and Hayden told her it was 'no big deal' because, "Lisa does that stuff for us all the time." Do you want to explain what he is talking about, young lady?"

I stood there paralyzed. Time froze. I froze. And so did my excuses. My brain wouldn't work. Usually a skilled liar, I went blank. Silence. I didn't even have the courage to deny it—my usual default. Instead, I just stood there, no different than Jared at the scene of the crime, staring at the floor.

"Well?"

She was coming toward me, two steps at a time, up the stairs. I moved back against the door to my parents' room.

"Well?"And "*Well? Is it true*? Did you show them your body? Did you take off your clothes for them?"

All I knew to do was nod. The one hundred "but they made me's" and "it was their idea's" weren't coming to my head fast enough. I was terrified that she knew even more than she was letting on. That she somehow knew of my secret plan to run away from home at sixteen and become a *Playboy* centerfold. I was mortified.

"I can't even look at you—spit flew from her mouth—You! Go to your room!" It was on the tip of her tongue. I felt it. She wanted to call me a whore or a slut or something, but she didn't have the heart. Instead, she kept it there, in her heart and in her mind. I felt lower than dirt returning to my room.

"Your father's gonna kill you!" she screamed, heading downstairs to grab the phone.

I shut my door, gulped, wiped away the tears that were now racing down my cheeks, and tried to tell myself that maybe it was better this way. If they knew I was nothing more than a future beauty queen gone bad, maybe they wouldn't be so hard on me. What would be the point?

It took precisely sixty-eight and a half minutes for Dad to march up the stairs. Dad never came home during the middle of a workday. Heck, the man overslept until 11 a.m. every day and certainly couldn't afford to be leaving work at two in the afternoon, but there he was. He called me into his room, where he looked at me like I was the scum of the earth.

"Is what your mother's saying true?"

I nodded.

He sat on the edge of the bed, on Mom's side. He motioned for me to drop my pants. I knew I was about to be spanked and took my place over his knee as he hit me harder than ever. I was wearing a pink leotard under my shorts that morning because I had ballet lessons later that afternoon. I found it a bit strange that he was punishing me without my pants on for not wearing pants in the first place. I knew better than to point this out. A beauty queen, maybe, but not a dumb one. His hits stung, but not nearly as much as the disappointment in his eyes. Bruises were nothing compared to the damage to my pride.

***

136

Self-Diagnosis: Self-loathing. Attention-seeking. Ashamed.

80 Bottles: Escape Artist
"My filthy fridge has nothing to do with beer."

Finally facing that I was married to an alcoholic willing to spit beer in my face wasn't the first time I wanted to escape my life. It was probably the hundredth. Remembering earlier plans to become a centerfold and the way I lost myself in books as a child, I eventually realized escape was my method of operation. In fact, if I was honest with myself, and Quaker Oates, I'd say escape was one of my tools for coping with situations I didn't like. If enabler was my title, my foundation was escapism. Mental escape gave me the means to manipulate my reality and live in denial. Physical escape was a whole other thing.

It was in the late 80s when my brother Robert—Robbie—began complaining of back pain at night. I had zero desire to admit to myself that something might actually be wrong with him. Instead, I rolled my eyes at him, telling him I was onto him. I knew the little shit had to be faking something. He just didn't want to go to bed. He was pulling a trick to gain Mom and Dad's favor in order to stay up past "The Incredible Hulk" and "Dukes of Hazzard." I was sure of it.

What I didn't envy was the surgery he needed a few months later. It turned out that Robbie had some sort of a kidney blockage. This blockage was causing his very real pain and he needed surgery at Boston Children's Hospital. I was petrified.

While my parents assured us he would be perfectly fine, I could see that he was rapidly losing weight and I was sure he was going to die. Kids died all the time. There was Denise Kimball in my fifth grade homeroom. She had leukemia and there weren't enough glitter-covered cards made during recess that could save her. My cousin, Heather, died at six from a kidney condition and I had my mind set that this would also be my brother's fate. The little brat had found one last way to get my parents' full attention. And I couldn't even hate him for it. I was too worried about what life would be like without him.

My parents didn't give us much information about Robbie's health. Nor did they prep my brother Mark and I for the impending visit from Aunt Martha. Martha was set to take over for Mom while she and Dad stayed at the hospital with Robbie. Convinced they would soon be picking out a coffin for my brother, I assured my mother I would behave for Martha and would keep an eye on Mark, and my toddler brothers, Jack and Josh. I knew how important it would be for my parents to focus on Robbie and I wanted to help. My intentions really were to help, not to run away. But intentions, well, let's just say they don't always translate well into action—not at that age anyway.

Martha arrived with an onslaught of suitcases. Had I not known she'd only be with us for a week or two, I'd have been quite sure she was moving in. Day one of Martha's visit was quite nice. She let us pick out anything we wanted for dinner—grilled cheese sandwiches—and spoiled us with a trip to the local ice cream stand, Walpole Creamery. *This won't be so bad*, I thought. *Maybe Robbie will be okay after all. Robbie hates ice cream anyway. This is perfect timing.*

But by day two, Martha had plans that didn't involve double-dipped frostys and rainbow sprinkles. Instead, she'd risen early that morning and taken a full inventory of the house. Particularly, the refrigerator.

"Oh, your *poor* mother," she exclaimed, crinkling her forehead and scrunching up her nose as she peered into the fridge. "She's been too busy to clean the fridge. She's been so worried about your brother."

Too busy since 1978, I thought. *How do you expect her to clean like that with so many kids and a husband who does nothing to help out?*

I'd never seen my mother clean a refrigerator in my life. Mom was not a housekeeper. She swore that cleaning house was a waste of time. After all, the house was only going to get messy again. And who could blame her? With four sons, a messy daughter, and a husband whose version of helping around the house was putting his own clothes in the hamper—Dad literally sought approval for this—she was outnumbered. When she had no other choice, of course, she'd do it. But that often involved enlisting me, the only girl, to help.

I sat at the kitchen table, missing Robbie in spite of him being a useless boy, and thinking about what I'd do for the day while Aunt Martha proceeded to unload the contents of our refrigerator on the kitchen counter. *Maybe I'll work on my fort with Lori. Or maybe I'll go swimming with Julie. Maybe today is a good day for making a stretchy rope with Julie that stretches the length of all our street. If we work harder, we can make it longer than last time. We were so close.* My daydreams were cut short by my aunt's words.

"Go and get a toothbrush from the bathroom," she said.

"Huh? Why do you need a toothbrush?"

"*I* don't need a toothbrush. *You* do," she said, laughing.

"I'm not done eating breakfast yet. I'll brush my teeth when I'm finished my cereal."

"You don't need the toothbrush for your teeth, silly. You need it to scrub out the fridge."

My jaw hung at its hinges. I'd heard of people cleaning with toothbrushes. I guessed they were good for getting in the small crevices of things. I wasn't sure, but what I *was* sure of was that I wasn't keen on the idea of finding out first-hand. *Does this woman have no heart? Tease a girl with Walpole Creamery and then stomp on her last two weeks of summer with toothbrush cleanings? What is wrong with her, anyway? Does she not know Robbie is dying, Mom and Dad haven't noticed me all summer, Jack stinks again, and I have better things to do than care about dirt my mother wouldn't notice if it was two inches from her face?*

They say oldest children are good for issuing guilt trips to. 'They' are right. (I admit, right here and now, I've made the same mistakes with JJ.)

After my protests, Martha looked at me and said, quite simply, "We need to do this *for your mother*, Lisa. She needs our help. You promised you would help her. I heard you."

The next seven days was filled with what I pegged "Traveling Toothbrush Chores." You'd be amazed at the places a toothbrush can venture: Under the rim of a toilet bowl, between the niches of a kitchen sink, under stove burners, behind counter tops, and so on. But on the seventh day, I'd been taught, even Jesus rested. On the seventh day, I crouched behind the couch, hoping Martha wouldn't see me. Breakfast wasn't worth it. I needed an escape from this crazy cleaning lady whom I was sure I could not possibly be related to. *Go away!*

Martha was helping Josh and Jack get dressed when I finally made my escape to Julie's house. I rode my three-speed pink Huffy as fast as I could. I was down the full length of my street in under a minute and neatly tucked in Julie's basement in under two. There, we spent the day playing with Barbie dolls and getting an impromptu lesson in sex education from her big sister, Heidi. Watching Ken and Barbie screw was far more entertaining than hearing about how my "poor mother" must just "not have had time" to do things I knew she hadn't ever considered doing. *Just how many times can a person clean the same closet anyway? Nawww. The cleaning-psycho-Aunt Martha won't miss me. And if she does? So what!*

I knew what I was doing when I did it. I knew Martha had no clue who Julie or her family was.

She'd have had to knock on every door in the neighborhood to find me. *Besides,* I reasoned, *who'd do that when they were busy shining up the wood and taking stock in Mr. Clean products anyway?*

Growing up in the 80s, at least before the Adam Walsh kidnapping case, parents were pretty free about letting kids play outside all day. The general rule for most of us was that you could go within a certain boundary—say, within a few set roads of your own street—but you had to be home by dark. All the parents in the neighborhood knew one another and watched out for each other's kids. Lunchtime was often a matter of whose house was closest. We often timed our play locations around whose mother had gone grocery shopping and who had the best snacks. Sometimes, we doubled up, telling neighborhood mothers we were starving and making sure to wipe crumbs from the last meal off our faces. We bounced from house to house this way, mostly unsupervised and rarely questioned by adults. Come dark, we all knew it was time to go home. If not, someone would come looking.

Julie's mother sent me home for supper just as people were turning on their porch lights. I was entirely clueless of Aunt Martha's now frantic and twelve-hour search for me. When I got in the door, she didn't need to give me a guilt trip. The look on her face said it all. The poor woman had been petrified.

"Oh! Thank *God*!" she flung herself at me. "I was just about to call the police! *Where* have you been? *Why* didn't you tell me you were leaving? I was so worried."

I didn't have the heart to tell her I had purposely escaped in order to give myself a day of Sabbath. Instead, I apologized, shrugged, and told her not to worry about me, I was a "big kid".

I'm not sure whether Martha was on to me about why I had "runaway" to the other end of the street that day, or if the house was just so sterile clean that there was nothing left to do, but she laid off on the cleaning after that and the rest of her visit was pleasant.

When I was finally able to visit Robbie in the hospital, I clung to my mother and demanded to know exactly when she was coming home—down to the hour and minute. When she did get home, I didn't roll my eyes nearly as much as I once had when she asked me to do tiny things, like clear my plate from the table. I've never cleaned anything with a toothbrush since, but I did find it entertaining to tell her just how many uses there were for toothbrushes. I had a new patience and respect for Mom's dustier version of domesticity. *What harm does moldy cheese at the back of the fridge really cause?* Certainly, I had a newfound appreciation for the other end of the street and the art of a well-timed escape plan.

Sometimes I wonder if drinking is just Jeff's way of escaping. I still do little things to escape my everyday life. Of course, it's nothing as dramatic as playing Houdini from the toothbrush caper, but there are still those little ways. Sometimes, to escape life, I do this quirky thing. I've done it since I was about ten. In tense or stressful times, I inhale deep, close my eyes, and picture myself and my life as the opening scene of a movie. Maybe that has something to do with the writer in me. Maybe I should be writing screen plays instead of working for a public relations firm these days.

It's the oddest thing, really. I do this most often when I'm bowling, of all activities. I don't find bowling particularly stressful, but for some reason, I find myself habitually doing this movie opening credit thing as I march up to take my turn. I walk toward the pins with a ten-pound bowling ball attached to my right hand, take in the loud music, and picture my audience gasping to see if I'll strike or spare.

I have no idea why, but when I do, I bowl better. It's almost as if having an audience somehow encourages me to focus, try harder, and yes—get that strike. I wonder if I'd be more successful if I had an audience for my life, someone to hold me accountable: Enter writing. I repeat this ritual when I'm driving. Religiously, I tilt my rear view mirror toward me, so I can see the top half of my face. Sometimes, I tilt it so I can admire my cherry glitter Bonnie Bell lip gloss. I always make sure not to tilt it far enough for a shot of my chins—plural. I wonder: *What would my life be like if people were watching, paying attention?*

I drive along, taking in the scenery and admiring my chocolate eyes, as I write an opening scene in my mind. I set the scene gently: "Thirty-something with oh-so-eccentric lip gloss heads out complete with Hello Kitty sequin, peppermint skull cap."

145

Not bad, I pat myself on the back, ignoring the devil on my right shoulder who reminds me that thirty-somethings are too old for miniskirts, glitter, and certainly anything Hello Kitty. I never get further than the opening credits of my vanity movies. I'm not sure if it's just that I feel silly or if I'm just too pleased with my own artistic license that I never move into a plot. It's probably a combination of both. The feeling of the whole thing is sort of like singing in the shower. You worry you might get caught, but in your mind, you are quite convinced you are the next American Idol. Trust me, folks, American Idol, I am not.

If my life *was* a movie, the primary plot might develop something more like, "Former giraffe geek-freak blossoms into eccentric artist wanna-be—taking risks she knows better than to take and being sure her children are free enough to do the same." Or maybe it'd be, "Jilted Love Goddess Reinvents Herself as Princess, Adored by All?" What about, "Fuchsia-Haired Soccer Mom Struggles to Find Identity of Her Own Despite Living with Oscar the Grouch?" Or maybe just, "Pink Big Bird Breaks Free." Drew Barrymore would most definitely play me in this movie. She'd drive that same yellow jeep from one of her older movies and wear a wild blonde afro wig. Of course, they'd probably have to put her in a fat suit, but no one would mind; it's Drew Barrymore. Really, the movie character I identify with most is the reliable man-beast otherwise known as Bridget Jones. From her big ass to her bigger white panties, how could I ever deny the similarities between Jones and I? But there's nothing wrong with dreaming about being played by the fair-haired Barrymore anyway, is there? *Would Drew really mind? Isn't acting supposed to be a stretch? At least the challenging roles? Pretty please? With sugar?* I wonder if Bridget was tortured by bullies like me as a child? I know she wasn't married to an alcoholic. Although even Mark Darcy certainly wasn't above an after work cocktail. *Hmmm.*

* * *

Self-Diagnosis: Lost in fantasy. (Because it's easier.)

79 Bottles: Are You There, Higher Power?
"It's me, Fat Ass..."

July 8, 2008
Dear Mr. J,

Heard a song on the radio today. "He ain't the leavin' kind" was part of the chorus. Or maybe that's the title. It doesn't really matter. I had to turn the song off. It was about God.

At Alanon, they speak of a higher power. They talk about surrendering your problems to God and that he's supposed to step in and fix things. That's where I'm having a lot of trouble here. I don't get why God would put us in this position in the first place. I know, I'm placing blame. It's God's fault he drinks? Come on, Lisa. You know better. Whose fault is it, really?

Alanon would want me to blame it all on Jeff. I can't do that. I see how he is when he's sober. I know the man inside of him. I see that he wants to be a good person. Hell, he is a good person when he's sober—for the most part.

His moods are getting to me pretty bad lately, though. He flips out about the little things. I think it's because he's irritated all the time when he isn't drinking. Everyday, there's a new reason to flip out. It's like he invents reasons to snap just so he can have an excuse to drink. It's like he's looking for a permission slip—not so much from me—but from himself. "My life sucks, so therefore, I have to drink and it's not my fault." I, of course, like an

148

idiot, go running to the store to make sure he has enough. I don't want to listen to a rage about why we are out of beer.

As for the blaming thing, I am no different than him. It's just another reason we're the perfect match. I say, "Jeff drinks, so my life sucks." I'm not a good Alanon person. He's an even worse AA person. He went to a meeting and walked out after ten minutes, telling me he could quit any time he wanted. Yeah. Right. And I wonder, could I?

As for surrendering to a higher power? I know I need God but I can't face him. I am sad. I am scared. I feel so fucking alone. I wish someone would come and give me a miracle. I wish Jeff would stop drinking and whatever hold that alcoholism has on him would just go away. But how can you face God when you know you aren't doing what you need? That you aren't really sorry, because it's too hard to change? I love you, God. I really do. I just wish I had the balls to face you. If I did, I don't even know where I'd look. Or, if I truly could.

***

Self-diagnosis: Coward.

78 Bottles: Sundays
"Manic Sundays."

I hate Sundays. I've always hated Sundays. Every Sunday, my parents dragged us to church. More accurately, my mother dragged us to church. Despite our protests, she managed to get us there just before the ending of the Homily and right before communion. Mark hated it the most and liked to hit me all the way to the church. My revenge was pinching him. We never told on each other. Mark wasn't a tattle-tale. The reason we were always late was because Dad could never get out of bed in time for the 10:30 a.m. or even noon masses. A night owl, he generally went to bed around 4 a.m. and waking up for church was never on the top of his priority list. Unfortunately, it was at the *very* top of hers. This caused weekly Sunday fights between my parents—a staple of my childhood. These fights served as bookends to our weeks and made Robbie and I physically sick with worry.

It was ironic, really. Despite his inability to get to mass on time, Dad was the one who said the rosaries and taught us about the magic in a novena. Mom, on the other hand, was more skeptical and would often confess her doubts about organized religion to me when he wasn't paying attention. I always felt good that I could be open with her about my own doubts. My father's devotion to the church, the Catholic church, was always a bit off-putting to me. While I admired his dedication, I didn't understand why he was so rigid in his belief that the Catholic faith was the "only faith." "What then," I asked, "about all the good people who happen to be Jewish or who don't believe in God at all? How could a just God send them to hell for not believing in him?" I never got a firm answer to that. I'm not sure Dad believed anyone who wasn't Catholic was capable of being a good person.

I was confirmed at the age of fourteen. I was told that this was my decision and only my decision. I was told a lot of lies as a child. Like the pleaser I was, I took the confirmation name Ann—after the Virgin Mary's mother. The whole ritual was nothing but a forced exercise in submission for me because I didn't feel I had a choice. I knew not being confirmed would break my father's heart. I could never do that to him. So, my sophomore year of high school was the year I marched up to the alter, looked at a stranger bishop and reaffirmed my commitment to the Catholic faith. *Honor thy mother and father, Lisa.* Another lie. Probably another reason I can't face God.

As I've grown older, my religious beliefs have evolved. I now consider myself much more spiritual than I once was. However, I don't like defining myself as anything other than Christian. I have several issues with the Catholic church. For starters, my childhood memories of religion are stained by the worst fights my parents—who believe it's better to stay married and miserable than to ever consider divorce, not much unlike me—ever had. While long ago Sunday scuffles are not the church's fault, I still resist any church's rigid intolerance of examination or doubt.

151

I also have issues with "services" I received from Catholic Charities when I was pregnant with JJ. Young, unmarried, and uninsured, Jeff and I were told by a woman with a cold stare that my "only option" was to give my child up for adoption. We hadn't gone to her for options—or had even wanted her unwarranted advice. We'd gone to the one place, like our parents had always taught us, where we would be safe, forgiven, and able to get help. We wanted guidance and hope. Instead, we were judged.

"You *clearly* can't *keep* that baby. You're too young. You aren't even married. What will people say? How will your parents feel? It will be okay, though. God will forgive you. You can both go to penance and I know a beautiful couple in the parish who is looking to adopt. You won't be a good mother," a woman, who I'd talked to for all of about three minutes had surmised of me.

Me? Not a good mother. Yeah, right. That's all I've ever wanted to be. We are engaged. My future husband is standing right here, you righteous bitch. Thanks very much, but you can keep your adoption papers. We don't need this shit.

To this day, I'd love to track that woman down and remind her of her own need for penance. *Only God can judge me.* JJ's Mother's Day card this year read, "I would never want any other mother but you. I love you very much and I'm so proud you are my mom. I love you even when I'm mad at you. Love, JJ." *Eat that, lady.*

Many times in my life I've searched for proof that God exists. Searching for a spiritual community to call home, I've had countless conversations and debates with agnostics, atheists, and pagans on this very issue. Try as they might to convince me of either no god or of other gods, I've reluctantly managed to stay close to my Catholic roots. Despite my poor experiences with the church, I've gone back to it many times, hoping my father is right when he says, "The people don't make up the church, Jesus does." *Yes and people suck,* I say to myself. I don't say this out loud.

The last thing you do when you attend an Alanon or Alcoholics Anonymous meeting is join together in a group of strangers, hold hands, and say the Serenity Prayer: *"God, grant me the serenity to accept the things I cannot change; courage to change the things I can; and wisdom to know the difference."* In each of these 12-step programs, the first step involves surrendering to a higher power—otherwise known as your version of God. I am not the only one who struggles with this first step. I have no problem surrendering my problems to just about anyone willing to take them on, but to sincerely offer up all of my problems to an abstract being has been particularly hard. While I believe, I don't think God has all that much time for my mini problems when there are things like AIDS, war, poverty, and babies with cancer to address. And if he does? Well, he's got his priorities screwed up. The god I want to believe in has his shit together. He has more pie charts, data sheets, and priority lists than the world has atoms. My little life? It isn't on them. I may have a hundred self-diagnoses from all the self-help books I've read, but narcissist is not one.

I explained this concern to a group leader once. She listened, nodded, and carefully suggested I look closer in the mirror. "How could the world have such a beautiful girl in it, one with so much love to give and so much pain in her eyes for her family, and there not be a god?" she asked.

I had no answer. I don't know about the "beautiful girl" thing or how the heck that woman could recognize the pain in my Hollywood sunglass disguise. What I do know is, if there's a stranger like that out there in the world, then the world might still be safe enough to surrender to.

For Jeff, step one was the easy part. It was getting him interested in taking any other steps to quit drinking that was difficult. Eternal opposites, Jeff never had an issue with religion or surrendering to God. His faith is, and always has been, unyielding. He hangs pictures of Jesus above our bed and throughout the house. He prays every night, never doubting. He makes no judgments on other people's beliefs but is never hesitant to share his own. He is not ashamed of his love of a traditional god and I admire him for it. Jeff's the guy you send to the door when the Jehovah's Witnesses come knocking. He's had more than one lively debate with them about religion. In fact, he enjoys it. He lets them in, offers them a drink and the use of our bathroom. I hide. Try as he might, he's never been able to convert them. But he's only in his thirties. He will, someday.

99 Bottles

ERIN LEE

***

Self-Diagnosis: Lost.

77 Bottles: Faith Chapel
"Random acts of faith."

Because of his interest in theology, Jeff has a habit of scoping out new churches and beliefs. We like to debate about them. He teaches me as much as he can, the way he's taught me to identify every breed of dog and say all fifty states in alphabetical order. Raised both Catholic and Baptist, he's never been too worried about the semantics of a religion. Instead, he's focused on its overall message. He's curious about what draws people to religions and likes to take the good from each faith he learns about.

There's an eclectic church he passes every day on the way to work. This church, Faith Chapel, is housed in a former strip club converted by Born Again Christians in the late 70s. It's well-known around town for its boisterous signs – oversized and so bright they make me think of Vegas. I like to imagine what the signs used to say, when the building was a seedy, less-than-gentleman's club. I imagine the women who danced in that church, with names like Brooklyn and Jewell. They remind me of my centerfold and I wonder where she is now. I can see her, dancing, on the alter-stage.

For now, its messages are like wholesome fortune cookies you look forward to reading like "Come to the Lord!" and "Fear Not: Only Jesus Can Save Your Soul!" Some are less serious, with jokes or reminders; even with words of encouragement to Jet fans before or after big games. I wonder, sometimes, if Jeff misses living in the bible belt as an army brat. I know he misses the Midwest. Faith Chapel's sign is like the billboards you see driving through Georgia. Maybe that's what first attracted him to the Faith Chapel and got him in the ritual of reporting each day's new message at dinner time. At times, that sign was probably the best part of his day.

Jeff and I were out doing errands early one Saturday morning when we drove past the church. Ready to read our thought, joke, or warning of God's rapture for the day, we were speechless, at first, when we saw it had been sprayed with graffiti. Vandals had written "Lies!" and drawn hate symbols on the base of the sign, which now read: "Mr. Vandal: God Loves You Too" at the top. I wanted to cry. Jeff pulled into the parking lot to get a closer look. Vandals had sprayed, in red paint, "There is no God" and "Hate" on the building itself.

"Holy shit, hon."

"I know," I managed to say, unable to speak more.

"Why would anyone do something like that?"

"I don't know. It's mean."

"I know."

"I think the people are in there," I said, motioning toward the building. "I mean, they must be. They already changed the message on the board."

"Let's go."

I knew exactly what Jeff had on his mind, as he pulled the keys from the car and started walking toward the open church doors. I quickly followed behind. When we entered the building, a man in his late thirties greeted us.

"Can I help you?" he said, twisting the hair in his auburn goatee and looking curiously at us.

"We saw what those jerks did," Jeff explained. "I used to be a carpenter. I'm good at fixing things. Is there any way my wife and I can help?"

The man exhaled, stopped fidgeting with his goatee, and smiled wide.

"That's so good of you to offer. We can't do anything until the insurance adjusters are here on Monday," he explained. "Then, we're going to have a community day to clean up the place. If you want, I could take your number."

"That would be great. Do you have any idea who would do this, and why?" Jeff asked.

"No. It will be okay," the man, who had by now introduced himself as the pastor of the church, replied.

"I just can't believe someone would do this," Jeff said.

"It's awful," I chirped.

The pastor took our information and we began walking to the car. He shouted to us as we opened our respective doors. "We have services on Sundays at ten. All are welcome."

Jeff and I smiled at each other as we drove away, taking one last look at the damage. Months later, long after the insurance adjusters had been by, we'd sneak over to the chapel together at five in the morning to fix up the patch-jobbed sign as best we could. By then, the community day had come and gone but no one had bothered to fix up the base of the sign. Since then, no more damage has been done to the Faith Chapel. While we've never attended services there, Jeff and I feel a special connection with that church and he still reports to me about the sign's new message. Today: "Today is the first day of your new life."

***

Self-Diagnosis: Grateful. Open-minded. Hopeful believer.

76 Bottles: Taking Control
"Facing my own issues."

Over the years, Jeff's rightly accused me of being a control freak. *Ya think?* It's me who counts the beers on the counter, isn't it? It's me who would argue about the validity of an entire religion's message based, simply, on one woman's attitude at a church-affiliated agency. I used to take offense when he implied that I had something broken inside of me. It's the things that are true that hurt us the most. God and religion weren't the only things that made me uncomfortable because I couldn't control them. There were others. I did everything I could to avoid or change those things. Other times, I wondered how it was possible for a control freak to live in a home with so little control. I justified this ability as love. I called myself a martyr.

Looking at my childhood, it's no wonder that when I finally did get out "into the real world" I chose a profession where I could hide from bullies. I picked a job where the power was mine, which only fed my compulsive need for control. Former bullies had to kiss up to me as a journalist; not the other way around. I relished in it; not much different than my friendship with the much younger Lori. In this sense, I got to play God—rather than believe in him—every day.

I always knew I'd be a journalist. At age thirteen, I worked as a stringer for a weekly rag in Brattleboro. I wrote a column on my hometown—comings and goings, weekly events. I enjoyed the job, despite being paid only thirteen cents an inch. I got a kick out of seeing my byline. That byline was a drug for me.

My job at that paper was the first of many, but I didn't always write to tell the news. Often, I wrote for me and me alone. This is where I had complete control. No bullies, no overbearing mothers, no boys who wouldn't look at me twice existed in Lisa's Journal Land. I wrote in notebooks, on napkins, and on the backs of envelopes. I toted pens and highlighters with me everywhere I went. When I didn't have paper, I wrote on my hands, legs, and wrists. I used—almost abused—writing as a way to deal with my emotions from a very early age. I started my first full journal at fourteen and writing became a lifestyle.

Later, I discovered one of many reasons for my obsessive need to write was a lifelong, undiagnosed struggle with depression. My first diagnosed bout came in 1996, shortly after meeting Farmer Charming. I found it frustrating and confusing that depression would strike when I'd finally met the man I'd been searching for. But Jeff was a trooper. He understood depression and took my declining stability seriously in our first years together. For several weeks, I attended intense therapy, including group therapy, to deal with ongoing issues I hadn't addressed.

Resistant to taking medication and fed up with counselors who didn't seem to care about anything but getting paid, I eventually convinced myself my depression was simply a fluke: Big mistake. From 1998 to 2002, I gave up on my daily journal and fun writing. While I was working professionally as a daily reporter at a 20,000 circulation paper, I wasn't putting creative energy into it and wasn't enjoying my work. My spark in writing was renewed, however, when—*Proof God Exists Number One*—Early Childhood Services began a poetry course for young moms who wanted to learn to write and chronicle their children's lives. My own mother had always kept a journal for me as a child and I planned to do the same for my kids. It was there, in a make-shift classroom, with about twelve tired mothers looking for the free food and childcare, that I wrote my first poem and fell in love with the written word all over again. I was lifted by the pen from my depression. I haven't stopped writing, or been clinically depressed, since.

Our teacher, middle-aged Annabel Rancelore, was a free spirit who nearly drowned herself in hippie dresses and vibrant scarves. She took a deep interest in all the women in the class, regardless of our abilities, and offered us endless ideas to inspire creativity in a less-than-creative setting. The first poem I reluctantly wrote was called *Dandelion Dance*. It was about my kids and how they liked to pick dandelions—which I'm highly allergic to— for me. During that time period, there was always at least four bud vases brimming with these flowers around the old farmhouse we were renting. I ate Claritin like Tic Tacs. "Mom," Nathan would remind me, "don't step on the pretty yellow flowers." He'd scoop them up in his tight two-year-old fist and present them to me.

After reading my first poem, flush faced, aloud to the group, I was hooked. I felt like I was sharing the innocent spirit of my children with a sympathetic audience. There, I was not judged and was pushed to explore my creativity. I began reading poetry as quickly and devotedly as I could. I took a liking to the realism and confessionals in the work of Sylvia Plath. I sympathized with her marital struggles and was drawn to her cynical way of alluding to her own issues. I liked that she didn't pretend to be perfect. I admired her. I knew what it was to be depressed. I knew what it was to live with a depressed person. And I knew, that for her, writing about it was probably as good a way as any to help her cope. That is, I "got" her and felt like she "got" me. This connection, however imagined, helped me want to write more.

Annabel and I were kindred spirits from the start. While we never talked about our personal lives, I could feel that she understood me and my poetry. I spoke to her of my need to "fix myself" and the long struggle I'd had in coming to accept God into my life. She encouraged me to journal about this, telling me that sometimes the best way to fix something that is broken is to look at the individual broken pieces. "If you just sweep it up, it's easy to ignore," she said. "If you look at the pieces, you might be able to find a way to fix them in order to put them back together." Her advice made sense, and so, I began journaling and writing poetry about my quest to fix not only myself and my marriage, but my relationship with a higher power. Even at work, in between the headlines…

***

Self-diagnosis: Write-a-holic.

75 Bottles: "Be The Butterfly"
"Those with the strongest wings fly alone."
-Anonymous

Years of journaling, often where I'd speak directly to God, turned into a silent spirituality for me. I talk to God daily now, but never discuss this with anyone. Like an imaginary friend a child would have, I believe God is by my side always. While still skeptical about formalized religion, there came a point where I needed to return to the church.

JJ and Nate were about to make their first penance. Ella was right behind with first Holy Communion only a few years off. Penance—also known as confession—is a sacrament in the Catholic church where we are asked to tell our sins to a priest. That priest, through God, absolves us from sin. When you walk out of the confessional, you are basically working with a clean slate—sinless and free of guilt. While I love the concept behind a fresh start with God, I don't like telling a human being—one with sins of his own—my personal misadventures. JJ and Nate were feeling the same way—nervous and skeptical—about telling the priest their sins. Hoping to ease their nerves, I used this as an excuse to go to penance myself. It was kind of like throwing myself out of the plane first, reassuring them (and myself) we all had parachutes.

"It'll be fine, guys," I said. "Trust me, whatever you have to tell the priest, I have worse. I'll go first and then he'll be distracted." *Yep. I've officially turned into Mom.*

"Bless me, Father, for I have sinned. It's been seven years since my last confession," I began. I sat directly across from a frail, white-haired Father Patrick. I twisted my fingers in my sweaty palms as I listed every sin I could think of. Seven years is a long time and I'm no angel. I told him of how I'd been away from the church since JJ was born. I told him why. I told him about the lady at Catholic Charities, Jeff's drinking, how I tried to antagonize Jeff in fights, how I was looking for an excuse to leave my husband, and how I was no good at this "for worse" part of the vows. *Why does that have to be in vows anyway? No one else seems to care. Look at Aunt Martha.* I even confessed my guilt in making my kids complete a sacrament I wasn't sure I believed in myself.

By the time I got to the smaller things—not stopping to help the lady with the blown out tire in the school parking lot because I was in a hurry and purposely not telling Jeff about a bill that I knew would set him into a foul mood—I was still looking at my sandals. Tears had soaked my yellow shirt and were now spilling down to my feet.

"Dear. Can I interrupt?"

I was startled to hear Father Patrick. I had almost forgotten where I was. I sat up straight, looking him in the eye for the first time. I used the back of my wrist to mop up fresh tears as he searched for a handkerchief. He handed it to me.

"Thanks."

"What's that on your neck?" he asked.

My neck? I looked down. A small yellow butterfly pendant was hanging from a fragile silver chain. Jeff had bought me this necklace the day we'd discovered the vandalism at the Faith Chapel.

"It's a butterfly," I said.

"No. It's you."

"It's me? I don't understand."

"You are a beautiful person, dear. I can see how deeply you love."

Tears came streaming back. I remembered the stranger lady from Alanon who'd called me beautiful. Besides Mom, not many people have called me that without prompting. But Father Patrick didn't mean the kind of beautiful I was thinking of. I knew that.

"I'm not giving you a penance. You've punished yourself enough. You need to stop. You need to see yourself as that butterfly. You were a caterpillar. *Now* you are evolving into this whole beautiful new creature. It's a transformation. I want you to go out and be that butterfly. I want you to stop beating yourself up. Jesus loves you. God loves you. You love your family and it's clear they love you too."

If I hadn't been falling apart, wasn't soaking wet from tears, and it hadn't been over forty minutes since I'd entered the confessional with a church full of people behind me, I might have hugged Father Patrick. Instead, I mumbled a quick, "Thank you, Father."

"Now, you can take this handkerchief with one condition," he said. "That is that you come back to the church. I need that handkerchief back. I want you to bring it to me after Sunday mass, okay? And bring those children of yours too."

I agreed. I walked out of the confessional holding my head high, imagining I had wings, smiled at the boys, and ignored the stares of other parishioners who'd been waiting—likely sure I'd killed someone. "Be the butterfly," I told myself. It became a mantra for me. *Did he just trick me into coming back to church?*

***

Self-diagnosis: Motivated for change.

74 Bottles: Blue Can Slam
"I don't know how much longer... It makes me sad."

When I blew out the candles on my childhood birthday cakes, I always wished for the same thing. Even at age five, I wished for a happy family of my own one day. I dreamed of being independent, without rules about how far I could ride my bike or in which order to eat dinner and dessert. I fantasized of a life filled with three children who I'd hug ten times a day, needed or not.

For years, I had a reoccurring dream that I was being chased by people wearing big yellow chicken costumes. My research on dreams tells me that I was running away from something in these dreams. Possibly, I was running away from myself. At the very least, I was running away from something unpleasant. I learned that chickens represent a feeling of powerlessness, cowardliness, gossip, or excessive talking. With this information, I can conclude that I felt powerless as a child and wished for autonomy even in my dreams.

I've never had chicken chase dream as an adult. I am not sure if this means I have stopped running or if I'm no longer motivated to run at all. *Have I accepted powerlessness?* To better understand these things, I created and I wrote.

Sept 29, 2009
Dear Mr. J,

Been working on my fairy gardens. Feels good to be creative and focus on stuff I care about, rather than beer. Things got really bad with Jeff last week. Promised he wouldn't drink for at least one week and he's already drinking again tonight. It's only been four days. I can't worry about it. Alanon would say this is not my issue. It's his issue. I called the cops on him. He hates me for it. I don't know how much longer we'll stay married and it makes me sad.

The fairies are keeping me occupied and making me feel better about stuff.

Sept 30, 2009
I heard a description today in an audio book by the woman who wrote P.S.—I Love You. *I think the book is called* Wish You Were Here. *It's a fiction no-brainer. However, it had this great description that I will "borrow" someday. She was talking about how her mother used to look at her in this disappointed way, but try to make it look authentic. She said something like, "She smiled at me one of those smiles where you can tell she's gritting her back teeth." I could picture that right away and I loved the description of it—a forced smile. A smile of obligation. I am living that smile.*

I've been a bit of a slacker when it comes to writing in my journal so I'm getting back to that (or trying to anyway). I'm finding most of my creative energy is going into my fairy gardens. I'm really enjoying those. Ella loves them. I love when she takes an interest and helps me. I worked on Winter Wonderland (Winter Dreams?) today. I am anxious for the clothes pins to dry so I can hang mini candy canes from it. I think I will use it to wrap Christmas cookies when I am finished. What a treat that will be.

It's getting harder and harder to go to work. Depression and anxiety are kicking my ass. The boys' sports schedules aren't helping. I am out every night with either football or soccer or both. I am thankful for the free time it's giving me to both write and listen to books on tape while they practice though—always a silver lining for Lisa, right? Is this ever going to get any better?

Ella starts a new art class next week. Maybe that will bring me some joy. I love seeing what she comes up with.

***

They say alcoholism is a progressive *disease*. I still struggle with the word 'disease'. Cancer is a disease because you don't have a choice. Smoking is a choice. Lung cancer, often the result of it, is the disease. But I digress: The whole progressive disease thing means that alcoholics continue to need to drink more and more to get their fix. What started as a six-pack-a-week habit in the early years of our marriage was up to a nine-at-a-time, every other day habit by the time 2007 rolled around. I lined the fridge with the nine beers so they'd be cold for him when he returned from work. He expected it and I knew better than to argue about it.

99 Bottles   ERIN LEE

Jeff, always a clown, took to making jokes about his drinking. He began calling his every-other-nightly ritual "the Blue Can Slam". His beer of choice was Labatt's Blue. The cans, and bottles too, are a cheerful, shiny blue. He made jokes about downing them—one in each fist, as quickly as possible to "escape life". I never found the jokes funny. Instead, I found it difficult to not be offended that he hated his life—the life we built and shared—that much.

Jeff's jokes didn't stop with the blue can slam. Instead, he made comments about wanting to take "dirt naps". A dirt nap was Jeff's way of saying he'd rather be dead than live his life. Of all hurt his drinking caused, I think hearing that hurt me the most. By 2010, I began counting the number of times Jeff would refer to wanting to die. He was averaging more than forty times a week. For someone who hates numbers, I found myself consumed with counting things. From the number of beers on our counter to the sum of the equation it translated into in regards to our relationship, I was always counting. While he told me not to, it was impossible not to take thirty complaints a day personally. *Was the life we'd created together really so bad?*

73 Bottles: Can't Argue Numbers
"Me and Mr. J."

Dear Mr J,
Jeff's a number's guy. Maybe this will help. Maybe if he can see it in black and white he'll realize how bad things have gotten.

Record of Jeff's Drinking Activities beginning Dec 21, 2009

December 20: Conversation about how he will go to AA (prompted initially by my being upset about his drinking the night prior and followed up by an email he sent me regarding this topic)...a promise not to drink again until after the holidays.

December 21: Nine beers

Dec 23: Nine beers, urinated in the garbage can next to the bed—tried to hide this from me, major stumbling, dirty looks, cleaning out garbage can, ignoring my questions about what was in the garbage can. I emailed him (to be received in the morning to find out if he remembered what had happened)—this all made me feel so sad for him and disgusted with him at the same time. As hard as I try to understand why he is doing this to himself, I don't. I also don't understand how he can say that the kids and I deserve better but continue to find any excuse to drink.

Dec 29: Eight beers

Jan 2: Having a hard time with cravings, but no drinking. Withdrawn and in his room.

Jan 3: Washing machine breaks, bad day with clinical schedules being canceled for school—Jeff drinks. No clue how much he drinks. He stayed away from the family and there were no fights due to his drinking. (The next day he told me he had drank nine.)

Jan 8: Comes home after a bad day at work. Insists he has to drink. Insists that drinking contributes to "quality of life". Bad stumbling.

Jan 11: I was away on a trip to Virginia. When he called I could tell he was drinking. I don't know how many he had.

Jan 16: Nine beers

Jan 24: Not sure how many. I think more than nine.

Jan 29: I worked. He drank.

Feb 2: Drank ten beers, erratic behavior. Circling the kitchen table, pacing, definitely nearing black out. Didn't bother to kiss Ella goodnight.

Feb 5: Sassy, our fish, died. He drank. Very grouchy and irritable. Yelling at kids.

Feb 9: Nine beers? Made Alfredo and was genuinely pleasant (for a drunk person).

Feb 13: Nine beers

Feb 16: Nine (or more?) not sure. No issues with behavior.

Feb 18: Another day. Another drinking night. So much for trying.

Feb 20: This is now getting out of hand. (Not that it wasn't before.) But look at how much closer the dates are getting, Lisa. Wake up. This isn't going to stop.

Feb 22: I guess it's an even day sort of thing at this point. The pathetic part? I still love him. And I still believe that he'll stop one day. For me and the kids. But how long is too long to put up with this? Nine beers. And at least we're heading into an odd day. No abuse, verbal or otherwise. Just "gone" and in another zone on another planet. Anywhere but here, with us: Where he belongs.

Tuesday, Feb 24: Me again. Him again. Nine beers. Even drove to the convenience store before he started drinking to be sure he wasn't shorted that one extra beer we didn't have in the house.

Friday, Feb 27: Nine beers

Monday, March 3: Nine beers

Saturday, March 8: Nine

Tuesday, March 11: Nine

Thursday, March 13: Nine

Saturday, March 15: Nine

Thursday, March 20: Nine

Saturday, March 22: While I was hospitalized for acute and severe asthma—nine or more. What if there had been an emergency at home? I need to talk to someone about this.

Monday, March 25: Night I came home from hospital—nine.

Wednesday, March 27: Nine

Friday, March 29: Nine

Saturday, March 30: Nine

Tuesday, April 1: Nine

Wednesday, April 2: Six beers

Friday, April 11: Nine or ten, very drunk—probably well over nine or ten. "I wouldn't touch you with an eight foot pole." Calling me every name in the book, JJ in the driveway when we went to leave—didn't recognize JJ and thought JJ was breaking into his car, huge fight, I took the kids away for the weekend because I didn't feel it was safe for me (or the kids after the JJ thing) to be there any longer.

Tuesday, April 15: Nine

Friday, April 18: Nine (or more). No issues.

Saturday, April 19: Nine

Asked to resign early from his job. Had called in sick one too many times. Not sure how much of this has to do with drinking or not. All of it is depressing is all I know. Fuck it, be the butterfly

Forgot several entries: Drank three times the following week and one or two more since then

Thursday, May 1: Nine

Saturday, May 3: Nine

Tuesday, May 6: Nine

Thursday, May 8: Nine

Saturday, May 10: Nine plus

Monday, May 12: Nine and a half. (I used half for the marinade to make dinner earlier.)

Thursday, May 15: Eleven

Saturday, May 17: Eleven

Tuesday, May 20: Not sure how many—at least nine. Would he sober up if he saw this shit with his own eyes?

Friday, May 23: At least nine.

I brought the list to Jeff. He shrugged. He asked me to tell him something he wasn't aware of. I walked away, wishing I had a quarter so I could call someone who cared. But, even if I did, I didn't feel like there was anyone I could call. They wouldn't understand.

***

Self-diagnosis: Horrible at math. Done with counting numbers that don't add up to anything anyway. Defeated.

72 Bottles: Check!
"Now what?"

After researching the signs and symptoms of alcoholism, I wasn't surprised to learn that Jeff had all of the classic signs of an alcoholic. In a way, it was a relief to me. It seemed, that if I could name his drinking problem and put a label on it, there may be a way to fix it:

Dear Mr. J,

I've been a busy lady. I figure I should know the facts before I try to hit him with them. So, here's a list of the things they say are indicators of alcoholism:

1. The drinker does and says things when he's drinking that he wouldn't say or do while sober. (He may say this to you, or admit he's said it to himself.)—Check! I mean, pissing in the trashcan does qualify, right?

2. He must drink at every social event, or it isn't fun.—Check! Only life isn't fun for Jeff. And he hates social events. I'll never forget the time I had to convince him it was okay to go to his mandatory work party because he'd be able to drink there.

3. He lies or makes excuses about how much he drinks.—Check! "It's not my fault you made me eat dinner so I had to drink more to feel a buzz."

4. He drinks when he said he wouldn't.—Check! Bad days at work are notorious for this.

5. He drinks and drives.—He doesn't do this. Thank God. But he threatens to. I've had to hide the keys on more than one occasion.

6. He sometimes can't remember what happened while he was drinking.—Check! All the time.

7. He spends money and time on drinking that he should have spent on school, work, or family.— Check! And he makes no apology for it.

8. He prefers the company of drinkers and may dislike non-drinkers.—No check here. He prefers to be alone, period.

9. He says he can cut back or quit drinking, but he never does.—Check! Ha! We could repeat this one, oh, three hundred times? I remember the time when he said it'd been "forever" (a whole four days) since he "quit" drinking. (After a promise that he would not drink again until the next major holiday.)

10. He says he can't have a problem.—He used to do this. Not anymore. He admits it now.

So, Mr. J: What do you think? Seven out of ten ain't bad. Damn. He's really messed up. Worst part? He knows it. Worse yet? He doesn't care.

Told him today I was planning to write a book about his drinking. He laughed at me. More like mocked me. Said, "I can't imagine writing a book about how lazy you are or how much you bug me." Part of me gets that. I mean, maybe I should just "get over it". But the other part of me—the part that has had to lift his two hundred pound ass out of the hallway and tuck him into bed or sleep with him while he's drooling all over me, or even take his threats and insults that he doesn't remember come morning—says screw that. Marriages always have their kinks, but when you live with an alcoholic? It's more like a knot: One that goes around your neck. One that doesn't offer the mercy of a kink. Sighing here because I no longer dare to do it out loud.

P.S.—Now what?

In all of this counting, researching, and list making, I feel myself slipping away. I don't sing in the car anymore. I don't care what music is playing when I'm bowling. I haven't picked up a pen in months. I know it's time to pay a visit to the dreaded Quaker Oates. She asked me once if I had fifteen minutes to tell someone who I was, what would I say?

"Fifteen minutes? That sounds like a hell of a lot of time to talk about yourself," I say.

She lowers her pen and looks up at me. "Go."

"What would *you* say?" I stall.

"Go."

"Fine. Okay. Well, I'm a writer and a mom. I work in marketing in mental health, which means I try to educate the public about mental illnesses. I am married and I like to read," I offer.

"And?"

I bite my desire to lunge over the desk between us and shake her. *What the hell else do you want from me? And what is the point of this? I had to pull Jeff off the deck last night after he passed out.*

Is that more important? It was twenty degrees out there...

"And that's it."

"I want to hear about *you*, Lisa. I want to know what you are passionate about. What makes *you*, you? What would other people want to know about *you*?"

Do I look retarded? I know what you're asking. I just don't have an answer yet. Give me a break. I chew on my fingernails, something I haven't done since college, before giving her the answer I think she's looking for.

"I want them to know that I'm doing my best to be the best wife and mother I can be."

Quaker isn't impressed. I can see it in her frowning forehead. She tells me I have homework to do, reminding me that we are all individuals and shouldn't define ourselves by the people we care for, love, or are obligated to. Instead, she says, we should have our own sense of self and identity that we are confident in. To diffuse what is surely coming next—an analysis of my childhood and why it is that I have no self-identity that fits her definition of healthy—I agree to write a three-page essay on what I want people to know about me and bring it to my next appointment. The following Friday, I call her office to let her know I am sick. *Maybe she'll forget about the assignment. It was stupid anyway. At least I can check counseling off my list.*

***

99 Bottles

ERIN LEE

Self-diagnosis: Completely undifferentiated. Sick of trying so hard.

71 Bottles: The Field Mouse Named Survivor
"Other kinds of hope."

Nathan's cat, Licorice, brought home her first field mouse today. She promptly placed it in his palm, looking up at him, as if to say, "Look at what I brought you, Dad." I will never forget his response. "Noooo! Lick-ee! Don't do that! That's so, so, so meeeean!" He cried as he wrestled the half-mangled mouse from her jaw. She looked at him, with a cross between irritation and confusion. He swatted her away and he ran toward me, holding up the mouse, and telling me it was still alive. Ella did what I wanted to do. She fled for her bedroom.

"We can save it, Mom! I *know* we can!"

I didn't know whether to jump out of my skin or hide behind the couch. One thing I have always feared is mice. Even seeing it in his palms, with tears rolling down his eight-year-old cheeks, didn't totally make the fear dissipate. There was, after all, a wild mouse about three feet from me.

It wasn't long until Nathan's baby brown eyes had me convinced it was time to get over my fear of rodents and help him to save the little creature. I quickly salvaged a plastic cake box from the garbage can and began poking breathing holes in its top. He ran down to his room, grabbing one of his favorite stuffed animals in one hand while still clutching the field mouse in the other. He emerged with scissors and cut the head right off of that stuffed animal. He made bedding and packed that cake box about as cozy as any outside mouse could ever hope for. I don't think he noticed it was twitching.

Tonight, he's sleeping upstairs. He's locked his cat in his brother's room and is laying vigilant by the mouse he's named Survivor. I'm quite sure Survivor is missing one eye. I'm more than sure the cat managed to break one of his legs. But he's breathing. And sleeping.

Part of me is tempted to kill Survivor while Nathan is sleeping, to put the mouse out of its misery. But another part of me wants to believe just what Nathan does, that the little bugger, who is actually starting to look sort of cute in a scary sort of way, will actually be okay.

I've promised Nathan that if the mouse makes it the night and appears that he will live, we will make a trip to Pet Co. to buy him a little cage and food and other treats. I don't know if I will have to make good on that promise. I hope so. For Nathan's sake. And for Survivor's.

"He's going to be ok, Mom. I know he is!"

I told him how proud I was of him for trying to save the mouse. He looked at me, rolled his eyes, and gave me his bravest, most grown-up smile. "Mom! If I'm really going to be a veterinarian, I have to be able to deal with things like little dying mice." Could someone tell me when God decided that if I was going to be a Mom, that I'd have to too?

Goodnight, Nathan. Goodnight, Survivor. (Fingers crossed.)

***

Self-diagnosis: Mother first, wife of an alcoholic second. Survivor.

70 Bottles: Bigger Worries than Beer
"Back to web MD."

My background in writing articles for the health beat gave me an in-your-face familiarity with the signs of a suicidal person. Because of this, I approached Jeff about his references to "dirt naps". When he was sober, he'd tell me that he did—indeed—wish he was dead. But he'd say that he felt "too guilty" leaving me alone with three young kids and assured me that he'd never "actually do it". Other times, when he was drunk, or well on his way, he'd threaten to hang himself in the backyard or drive his car into a tree.

At some point in 2009, I asked him to stop making suicidal comments in front of the kids. I didn't want them to think it was a remote possibility. I didn't feel it was fair for them to worry about their grown father. They were, in fact, only children. They had a right to worry free childhoods. His idle threats certainly weren't conducive to that. He agreed and promised not to do it anymore; a short-lived promise.

Sept. 5, 2009
Dear Mr. Journal,
Dr. Phil talked about something called "Explosive Personality Disorder" today. I am wondering if that is what Jeff has. I am going to look into it. I need answers.

Mom is worried about me and I hate it. In a way, I wish I hadn't told her. In a way, it's a relief to have someone to talk to about things. I wonder if she'd start sending me poetry words again. I know that would help me, being accountable to a reader—anxiously (or at least good at faking it) awaiting my next work.

I'm watching an episode of "Secret Lives of Women" with a girl named Lexis who was getting into Poison's *back stage shows just by dressing "like a freak". She describes herself as an outcast: A former one, anyway. She literally pan handled for hair dye. She was on her own, pan handling, eating out of trash cans, and sleeping in abandoned buildings for years. But she ultimately pulled it together. She is a survivor.*

Mom called me a survivor today. Reminds me of Nate's mouse. It made me feel good—for a moment—but the guilt quickly consumed me. The last thing she needs is to be worried about me right now.

I wish I could come out with all of it and let her know I am okay and will figure things out like I always do.

Jeff seems to be trying to make an effort today. Part of me pities him. Part of me wants to hug him.

I don't know if there is anything left to save. Mom said she didn't want me to "just survive". I assured her I wouldn't let that happen. But I don't know how much I actually believe that.

I want to write poetry but my well seems to have run dry, so to speak, today. I mean, when you de-

scribe your poetry block with a cliché, you know you are in trouble.

Such is life.

I'm going to look up Explosive Personality Disorder now and see what I can find.

And later,

What I've found is not accurate when it comes to what I think he is going through. I'll write more on why I don't think it applies when I'm not so tired. I did find something referred to as Intermittent Explosive Disorder. It falls into the Impulse-Control Disorders category. The most common characteristic of this disorder is the inability to control aggressive or violent impulses. Once they act out the aggression they are feeling, the person may have a strong sense of relief because the episode happened, but will regret what they have done during the episode. The impulses the person feels will result in very serious assaults and/or property destruction. One example of what someone may do before and during an episode is the threat of or actually physically harming someone and breaking things of value to "hurt" their victim. Some people suffering from IED will express violent behaviors ranging from physical assault all the way to homicide or violent suicide. A diagnosis is made when several episodes occur in a determined amount of time.

Several resources I read while researching this also stressed that these episodes happen without being under the influence of drugs or alcohol. This makes me think of his road rage. Some symptoms the person may feel leading up to an episode is an intense feeling of wanting to hurt something sometimes with no legitimate reason for being upset, intense irritability or rage, an increase in energy, and racing thoughts. One report I read stated, "Some individuals may also report that their aggressive episodes are often preceded or accompanied by symptoms such as tingling, tremors, palpitations, chest tightness, head pressure, or hearing an echo." He's talked about that. About palpitations and even echoes.

I don't know. I'm not a doctor. Jeff's better at this shit. If only he cared about his own "disease". How can it be a disease, by the way? I mean, he chooses to pick up the beer, right? People don't choose cancer.

Who cares? I need sleep and I'm exhausted. It's not like he's going to listen to me or get help anyway. I'm going to make myself sick trying to cure him. I deserve better than that and so do the kids. Or, maybe I just need to get out of the mental health field all together. How many suicide feature stories can a girl write without becoming paranoid? Maybe that's all it is. I hate suicide. I hate everyone and everything.

***

Self-diagnosis: Wannabe doctor/shrink.

69 Bottles: Lola
"Embracing my inner gypsy queen."

Adulthood hasn't deterred my ability to escape into fantasy. I'm an expert at it now. I've had practice. In my single life fantasy, I live in a loft-style apartment in an old mill building overlooking a grand downtown. The city I live in is a small one. It's artistic and eclectic. On Friday nights, there are Art Gallery Walks and there is always a poetry reading going on somewhere. I live with two cats in this fantasy—Sylvia and Jane. Sylvia is black and dark and Jane is white and Persian. Both have personalities of their own and both are so smart they are almost able to talk to me when I come home with one man drama or another.

Friday nights are Chinese food nights. Saturdays are for sushi. Sunday is for sleeping in and not bothering to shower. I write on Sundays and Sylvia and Jane curl up in my lap while I sleep. I don't go out much on weekends, preferring to mate with a good book—deep in someone else's love story or drama; away from my own.

My loft walls are lined with bookshelves of poetry and writing books. I have a hard oak desk facing the busy front window of my apartment, overlooking the street. One wall is made from brick, painted white. I stare out onto the street while I write—the window cracked and my patchouli incense smoke billowing out of it as I sip on red wine. When I am bored or fidgety, I slip on some comfy moon boots and walk outside—being treated to the sounds of the city and inspired from the smells coming from coffee houses and local breweries.

This place I describe is similar to Main Street in Brattleboro, VT. Jeff always hated Brattleboro. In my single life, I work as an associated press reporter and a freelance magazine writer. Based at home, I set my own schedule and work out of my apartment. I write all night and roll out of bed around noon. An automatic tea maker helps me to get my days started as I call in for stories and assignments. Often, I am able to come up with my own assignments, using the people and character of my place to lead me to interesting tales.

The men I date in this life are attractive and interesting. They are artists and creators. They understand creativity and are interested in things like the theater and photography. They prefer black and white photography—developed old style in a dark room—to digital high tech artwork. They are graphic designers, advertisers, and writers. These men think outside the box and are not adverse to going to vegan buffets or trying out the latest juice bar in town. They are cultured and have more audio books than they do music albums on their iPods. They view tattoos as art and most have full sleeves of ink on their arms. These men are liberal but not so outspoken about it that they are obnoxious. They are able to see two sides to things and don't view the world as simply black and white.

In my single and childless world my nickname is Lola. I don't know why I am so attracted to this name, but I think it suits me. At least it suits me in this fantasyland. Lola is the kind of person who listens to National Public Radio and gets tattooed on a whim. Lola prefers acoustic music and live bands in small bars to rock concerts in atriums. She marches to her own beat and is not afraid to let anyone know it. Lola makes no apologies and has no one to answer to.

***

Self-diagnosis: Dreamer. (Maybe he is right about me.)

68 Bottles: What *Do* the Neighbors Think?
"...and why, exactly, do I care?"

Dear Mr. J,
May 29, 2010
Chris came over today. (Chris is a friend of Jeff's. Jeff met him doing work on Chris's farm as a second job to bring in extra money). *He was here to pay Jeff for his last day of work. When he got here, Jeff was so drunk. I mean, he was a hundred percent off his rocker drunk. I wonder if he is embarrassed by this. They are still outside now, talking. I wonder if Chris realizes just how drunk he is. I wonder if Jeff even cares. I am mortified. Jeff is such a good person. It's incredibly sad to see him like this. I never wanted to feel like this. I never thought I'd be embarrassed of my own husband, but I am.*

Before Chris got here, Jeff was wondering around the house in a drunken haze. It's been a quiet day. I'm thankful for that. But I suspect guilt is what brought Jeff to ask me if I wanted to play Bocce with him and the kids. I shocked myself by saying no. I was in the middle of a good book—one that might help me with weight loss. I didn't want to play Bocce with a drunken mess. I don't recognize him when he drinks like this. It's funny, I should. He's the Night Crawler. I know the Night Crawler well. Only, it's not night.

99 Bottles

ERIN LEE

It used to be that he would only drink at night. It gets earlier and earlier. Weekends are the worst. I dread them. They mean watching him fumble from room to room. They mean trying to shield the kids from just how drunk he is. And when he drinks during the day, he wants to be outside. I cringe at the thought of the neighbors seeing him clumsily throw a football to the boys. Or, what if he misses when he's pushing Ella on the swing? I guess it shouldn't matter. Who are they to judge? But it does. To me. And I wish it did to him. I miss the days when he was more secretive about it. The days when it embarrassed him to go to the town recycle yard with three cases of empty beer cans. Now, he just shrugs and tells me it's none of their business.

I hate my life. Even more, I think, than he does.

Note: Two years later, Chris's wife left him for another man, citing not being able to "live with a drunk" as her primary reason. I wonder if she ever wondered, "What will the neighbors think?" Honestly, I never even knew. I was too worried about what she might think of me.

***

Self-diagnosis: Just like Mom. Worried about the neighbors. Ugh.

67 Bottles: Love & Hate
"For worse."

The distance between two people increases with time when substance abuse is part of the equation. Evenings laughing together during "Everybody Loves Raymond" on the couch are replaced by the alcoholic locking himself in the bedroom to get blitzed while the sober parent helps the kids with homework and figures out what's for dinner tomorrow night. It only makes that gap bigger when the two people are natural opposites.

The world is divided into two types of people. There are those who face problems head-on and those who go into denial and pretend problems don't exist. The first spend their nights contemplating solutions while the later live in fantasylands. Jeff says I am a dreamer and that I don't face my problems head on. He claims he's a head-on person who never lets a problem go unresolved. While I admit this about myself, I also think he's wrong. I believe that I'm sober and, because of the very nature of sobriety, I *am* facing my problems head-on. While I use fantasy to cope with my reality, I am the one who sits up at night worrying that the kids will smell the beer he's knocked on the floor. I see *him* as a person who goes into a denial in his own way. Each night when he gets his buzz on, he's denying: 1. What he is doing is very wrong for our family dynamic and for himself, 2.

That beer and his buzz aren't going to solve anything, and 3. Reality.

Calling Jeff out on this philosophy is never a good idea. A man who prides himself on dealing with facts and analytical thinking, it does not suit his personal narrative to believe that he uses beer as a way of denying everyday problems that all adults face. This has made the distance between us even wider. To close it, I take the easy way out and tell him he's right; I'm the Queen of Denial. And he's Mr. Fix-It. It's just easier that way. In keeping him calm, I reason, Mrs. Fix-It gets a sober house for the night. And maybe, if she's lucky enough, she even gets to cut that distance between herself and the man she loves a few feet. Still, with an alcoholic, even millimeters can seem like miles.

January 9, 2008

I don't know where to begin today. I'm having a hard time seeing hope in any of this. Our anniversary is coming and I dread it. Why would I want to celebrate being married to a person I don't recognize? Why would he want to celebrate being married to me? He says I'm fat. I am. He says I'm lazy. I am. He says I am a disappointment. Tell me about it. I don't know what we're going to celebrate.

But one thing I do know? I know how he'll celebrate. He'll celebrate with those hideous blue cans. He'll laugh about it. He'll get sloppy drunk. And then, he'll expect me to have sex with him. He won't get off. He'll just sweat all over me. His sweat smells like beer when he's drunk. I hate it. I hate it all. I hate him.

The next morning? He'll be chipper and unaware. He won't have any idea what happened the night before. And he'll expect me to be that Sunshine character that he knows and loves who always has a smile on her face and is ready to go.

Sometimes, I just want to run away. I can't keep trying to fix something that isn't going to fix itself and that I can't fix alone…

March 10, 2008
Dear Mr. Journal,

I wish he'd just go away. I've been keeping records for months now on his drinking patterns. It's starting to feel pretty stupid now. I mean, what's the point? He's going to drink and he tells me he's never going to stop. He blames me, the kids, and his "hard life" for this. I blame his weakness. He's so strong in other ways. In this way, he's the weakest person I know and it makes me sick. I used to respect him. I mean, really respect him. I thought of him as some sort of Superman. I don't know exactly what he was rescuing me from. I don't even know if I needed rescuing back then. But now? What I wouldn't give for a rescuer now. But who would even want me?

I can't write tonight. It's too fucking depressing. Thanks for being here to listen. I think I'm going crazy. I miss having a best friend. I miss normal days. I miss normal nights. I can hardly remember what those are like. I need to find an escape.

***

Self-diagnosis: Far too sober. Opposite of dreamer.

66 Bottles: Quoting It
"All things alcohol."

"For most normal folks, drinking means conviviality, companionship, and colorful imagination. It means release from care, boredom, and worry. It is joyous intimacy with friends and a feeling that life is good. But not so with us in those last days of heavy drinking."

– Alcoholics Anonymous, *The Big Book*

***

Self-diagnosis: Helpless to do anything to stop this bullshit ride I put myself on. I get it. Sick of talking, reading, and writing about it. Need a break.

65 Bottles: Dad, the Classic Enabler
"Three strikes: You're out! (Or not.)"

If being an enabler is genetic, I know who I got it from.

On the way to Nana's house was an eccentric but modest home. It was painted a landmark purple and winked as we passed by. *Just a half hour more until Arby's*, I'd assure myself. To help us pass the time, and surely as much to help avoid Mom's disapproving glare, Dad made up trivia games on the long ride. These games always started at the purple house. He'd ask us questions on what various street signs and signals meant. The first to answer what a double yellow line meant got a point. The quickest to point out the purpose of a yield sign got two points. The game paid off in dividends years later when I didn't have to study for my driver's test and managed to get a hundred percent on the written exam.

The monotony of the drive was broken up by our visits to Arby's. I'd always order the same thing— roast beef melt with barbeque sauce, a strawberry shake, and a small fry. But Arby's didn't come cheap. We had to *earn* Arby's during the first half of the trip to "qualify" for such a treat. Constant fighting between Robbie and I made Dad institute a "three strikes" policy early on in our monthly ventures to Nana's. To earn Arby's, a person could not have more than three strikes. Strikes came from behavioral infractions such as trying to poke each other's eyeballs out, screaming, shrieking, biting, hitting, spitting, and pretty much anything else we could think of to make driving miserable for my father.

I always managed to earn at least three strikes by the time we hit the edges of Pennsylvania. Fortunately, Dad was forgiving—or at least that's what I credited him for at the time, now, as a parent myself, realizing he had an *obligation* to feed us dinner—and allowed me to earn "strike erasers" for prolonged periods of no strikes. As silly as the game seemed, it got us through these long and windy trips. The second half of the trip was always the worst, with Arby's digested and only more squabbling from the front seat for us to listen to. On the other hand, we now had no reason not to bite and torture each other, so we often turned into mini vampires on part two of the journeys. Still, Dad forgave us and gave in: My first coach in enabling.

***

2011

I inch the bedroom door open, expecting to see him sleeping. Jeff worked a sixteen-hour day today. He rises from his knees at the foot board of our bed.

"What are you doing?" I ask.

"I was praying for JJ," he says. He looks almost guilty. But the red marks on his knees tell me he's being his honest, true self. *This is the guy I fell in love with.*

I swallow and scold myself for thinking he'd blown off his obligatory fifteen-year habit of a good night kiss. *Why do I always think the worst? I have to stop it.*

"I'm worried about him too." I offer it like a white flag, though there is no fight on the horizon.

"I'll talk to him in the morning. It'll be just the two of us. He'll have to make a choice. I can go to practice with him tomorrow or I can go to his game on Friday. I feel so bad for the kid. He has no guidance."

"He has you, I plead. *Don't you know how much we all need you? Don't you realize how important you are to all of us? Why can't you see that?*

Jeff's brow is furrowed. He studies my face. I stare back.

"He has me from far away." Jeff's referring to his strict work schedule, which often keeps him from the kids' games and practices.

"That's not true. He has you right here. You have to earn a living, hon."

He shrugs. "I'll talk to him in the morning."

A typical type-A oldest child, not unlike his father, JJ has had a difficult day. Today was his first soccer game. His team lost, with a final score of five to zero. Moved from his usual position on the forward line, he's been placed by a new coach in the midfield as a halfback—a position he's never played. The best player on his team by light years, and I'm not just saying that because I'm his mother, he's frustrated that he has no one on his team he can trust.

"I pass the ball and the idiots don't know what to do with it. It's like they are aliens or something who have never seen a soccer ball before," he says, crying.

I've seen the kid cry only a handful of times since he was six. I'm uncertain what to do or say to help. I know more is bothering him than his soccer team. *How couldn't it be? Look at the chaos he's living in.*

JJ is shaking. He swats away his tears, as if they don't belong there, as he continues.

"I can't fucking do this anymore, Mom! I have *zero* time to myself. Just because I'm in honors math they decide that now I'm in honors English. And ninth grade French is not even close to reasonable. I'm a middle schooler."

I see Jeff in JJ's frustration. I press my lips together tight and let him continue. I want to reach for him and hug him but I remain planted on the couch, where I know he needs me to be for the moment.

"The coach is an idiot. My teammates are idiots. How do eighth graders not even know how to do a legal throw in? How is that even possible? I'm supposed to carry a team and figure out a way to get to Harvard like ten years from now? I can't do this, Mom."

He lays his head on the kitchen table. The tears have stopped, but the back of his neck is as red as the apples that grow in our backyard. I move to rub his back. He springs up.

"No! Don't *baby* me. Tell me the truth, like you *always* do. Tell me the *truth*. How did I play today, Mom?"

I sigh. "Well, you didn't play like yourself, hon. But you really did a great job. You aren't working with—"

"No. Don't make excuses for me. Tell me what I did wrong."

"Well, you didn't play aggressively, J. You held back or something. I'm not the expert here. You know I'm clumsy. Your father would be able to tell you better. He said he's going to come to a practice and help you learn the new position."

JJ looks up from the table. His number five ever-green Panthers jersey hangs around his neck. He peeks up from a stack of books.

"Yeah. Maybe Dad can help."

I know by the tone of his voice that he's decided the conversation is over. I also know, from dealing with teenagers and having been one myself, that pushing the conversation would be fruitless. After suggesting that he drop a class or quit one of the two soccer teams he is playing for and being denied, I walk away to heat up his supper—cube steak and corn on the cob. He gobbles it down as I retreat to the couch to write. *I'll talk to Jeff about it later. This kid has way too much stress for a thirteen-year-old.*

JJ is mumbling about how negative eight cubed times something can possibly equal thirty-five. I offer to do his English assignment for him.

"Mom, I can't have you writing my papers for me at Harvard. I have to do my own work."

I return to my writing that night and analyze the day's events and come out with some very important observations: 1. JJ is more like his father than I realized—his own worst critic who pressures himself more than anyone else around him does, 2. I am an enabler even with my own children, no different than Dad. *(Is it genetic?)* 3. JJ respects his father's opinion—at least when it comes to sports—more than mine; a good reason to have Jeff around, 4. Though he doesn't always show it in obvious ways, Jeff loves the kid more than I could ever ask for. It would never have occurred to me to pray for him, and 5. I can't fix every problem that comes my way, no matter how much I want to.

I write this list in my journal. I reach behind the couch for the remote, tucked in its normal nesting spot, and flip on the television. I don't feel like writing tonight. I don't feel like thinking tonight. Tonight, I will just be numb. I decide I will lay off of JJ and let him decide how he wants to handle things. I will let Jeff be his father without interfering. I will trust in each of them to get through their own stresses without meddling.

This isn't as easy as it sounds. It's well past 3 a.m. before I finally slip into bed. Jeff's snoring and I'm worried my tossing and turning will wake him. He didn't drink tonight, having arrived home so late from the business meeting and spending the only awake hour he did have praying for his son. My leg twitches. My toe cramps. I have to pee. I should be doing laundry. *Maybe if I made JJ a really nice lunch. Maybe if I called his teacher. May-*

be. *Or, maybe, I could just learn to butt out.* Finally, I drift off to sleep. *Maybe,* I tell myself, *I can come up with an answer in my dreams.*

***

Self-diagnosis: Helpless.

64 Bottles: Talking it Out
"Counting change."

By the time I got around to letting them in on our secret, I knew that my family thought I just wasn't interested in spending time with them. I had, in fact, made excuses for years about why we could not attend this function or that. What I was unable to tell them was that I had to stay home from many of these events to cater to Jeff's addiction. Whether it be to make sure he didn't drink or to carry him to the bedroom when he did, his alcoholism pulled me from my life. It took many years to bring me to a point where I could no longer keep them in the dark and knew I needed to open my mouth. As much as it would sting, I knew I may also need their help. With my independence at risk, I slowly opened up to my parents and siblings about my situation.

June 12, 2010
I asked him, and I'm hoping it's for the final time, if he thinks he will ever stop drinking. He says he never will. He's giving you your answer, dumb ass. He's telling you it will never be different. So, what are you waiting for?

Talked to the kids today about what it would be like if we split up. Without a job, it's hard to imagine how I will even do it. (I was laid off from my job as the agency public relations manager at a mental health agency in January of 2010 when the economy was at its worst since the Great Depression and unemployment rates were to the moon.) *I have to find something quick. Even if it doesn't pay a lot. I'm amazed at how mature they are about this. JJ said he's good with whatever I decide, as long as he gets to live with me. Nathan is good with whatever I decide, as long as he gets to live with JJ. Ella didn't say anything. Instead, she shrugged. And, in talking to Jeff about it, he fully admits he can't take care of the kids. "I'm a drunk," he said to me. It made me sad to hear him say the words out loud. I don't know why. I mean, it's not like he's telling me something I don't know. I guess it was because I wanted to hear him say, "I'm a drunk and I am going to do something to change it." Instead, he just stated it as a matter of fact. "I'm a drunk. The kids need to be with you."*

How does a man—a person—not fight for their kids? How does this man, the one I chose to have kids with, not even care what happens to them? How can a silly drink be more important? I can't get my head around this. I can't respect it. And if I can't respect it, I can't respect him. So, isn't that the answer to my question? You can't respect him. He doesn't care. He won't stop. He's done pretending he will stop. You've talked about it. Everyone is okay with it. So, what are you waiting for? It's time to leave.

I think this is where I have a problem. Why should it be me who leaves? It was not me who left our marriage. I didn't check out emotionally. I stayed here, firmly planted, believing in a man who no longer believes in himself. So why am I the one leaving? Why should the kids leave the home they love? Why should they be displaced? They are doing so well in school. They deserve better than that. It's him who should be leaving.

He uses his income as a form of control. This is a man who was never controlling before. Now, because I have no income, he's made it impossible for me to just walk away. I know he knows this. We've talked about this. I feel so helpless.

I've told Mom about my problems—some of them anyway. She's sympathetic. But I still worry about being judged. She doesn't seem to be judging me and that feels good, but it hurts to admit failure. I signed on to this marriage thing for life. To do anything less seems so weak. Or maybe I have that backwards. Maybe the weak thing is to continue to do this life sentence—for a crime I did not commit—and let the warden rule my life, my moods, my fears, my weight, and my mental stability.

I need to make a change and that change needs to be about me, and me alone. I just don't know where to start.

***

Self-diagnosis: Contemplation stage of change.

63 Bottles: Cutting through Cross-talk
"Can we pass notes?"

Alanon meetings ban something called "cross-talk." That is, when a person shares their story, others in the room are not allowed to interrupt or offer feedback. One person speaks and then the floor is passed to the next person. I always found this anti-constructive. For me, a reason to go to Alanon meetings was not just to hear others stories, but to get feedback on the issues I was facing in my own life from people who understood. This didn't happen unless I stayed after meetings and talked privately to group members—something I wasn't comfortable with doing.

Aside from a few close friends, I had very little people to talk to about the things we were experiencing in our home. The shame of it was nearly unbearable for me at times. I knew, from an intellectual standpoint, that I had nothing to be ashamed of. It was not me making the choice to get drunk every other night. That was on Jeff. But I wondered, was it something that had to do with me—something I should be ashamed of—that made him drink in the first place? I tortured myself with these questions, looking to food, cigarettes, and my journal for answers.

I wondered, was I not a good enough homemaker? I'm still one to sweep crumbs under the refrigerator. And we all know about my aversion to toothbrush cleanings. *Did I not make enough money?* Unemployment isn't exactly lucrative, but it wasn't like I was unemployed very often. *Am I not pretty enough?* Can a girl really have too many chins? And why *isn't* monthly acne at middle age cute? *Is it that I am gaining weight?* The look-in-the-rearview-mirror-and-flirt-with-yourself quirk wasn't working anymore. I was now a game show: "Who wants to bang an overstuffed snowman?" *Is that what's making him so miserable? Um, yeah, dumbass,* I told myself. *All of the above. Who* wouldn't *drink? This is all your fault.*

I finally went to him with these questions. He insisted that none were the reasons he drank. Instead, he said he used alcohol as a way of escaping from the stress of the responsibility that comes with having a family. He drank to avoid worrying about the work piling up on his desk. He drank so he didn't have to think about the mortgage or the faulty brakes on his thirteen-year-old Chevy.

No matter how many times he told me I wasn't the reason, I had trouble believing it. After all, I had work on my desk to dread. I had the same bills and financial responsibilities. I also had the added stress about wondering if my husband would be drunk by seven each night and how to shield the children from it. So, if these were reasons to drink, why had I not turned to the bottle myself? *It has to be something more. Why won't he tell me what it is?* I had to find out.

***

99 Bottles

ERIN LEE

Self-diagnosis: In need of answers.

62 Bottles: "Then Leave Him, Ma." "Mothering regrets."

I fell into a pattern of using JJ as my confidant about Jeff's drinking. Initially, I reasoned, it was important to be forthcoming with my preteen about what was going on in our home. He could clearly see that Jeff was drinking. I figured it was better to be open with him about these things than to keep him sheltered. He was a kid who valued the truth at all costs. Still, in hindsight, I made a mistake with this. He'd roll his eyes and make statements like, "What do you want me to say, Mom? If you're that unhappy, then leave him." These comments always jarred me. "But wouldn't you be sad? I mean, he's your dad," I'd insist. "Yeah, and he'll always be my dad, but he's a grown up and he chooses to drink. That's up to him. So it's up to you to decide what you want to do about it." *Ah, the wise words of a child.*

Jeff knows I talk with the kids about his drinking. Generally, he shrugs, writing it off as another sign of my need for constant communication. He says he has no idea how to be a father because he didn't have a decent role model. Emotionally missing in action and sometimes physically abusive, his own father was more worried about making money than the emotions of a sensitive kid he not-so-secretly worried would turn out to be a "faggot." As an adult, Jeff views his father with different eyes. A man he once feared, Jeff now pities him.

I view him differently. Roy is not an evil man. He is quiet and the type of man you wouldn't even notice in a room unless he was standing next to you. At 5'8 and 170 pounds, I have trouble picturing my six-foot husband ever being afraid of him. A big drinker in his younger days, I've never seen Roy even sip alcohol since meeting him in 1996. An intellectual with a passion for gardening and crime novels, Roy and I shared common interests and got along well. Handsome for his late-in-life age, Roy's quiet calmness is in direct contrast to the high strung and abusive man of my husband's childhood.

Bi-yearly visits to Jeff's parents' house always go the same. I sit in the kitchen while his mother cooks and Jeff follows Roy around the house looking at whatever project he's just completed. There's a silent competition between the two of them, who often compare their gross incomes and mortgage rates. I don't understand it. I assume it's a guy thing and hope my sons are never like this with one another or their father, but I suspect they will be.

I've never been comfortable during visits to Jeff's parents' house. While his mother is more than hospitable and his father someone I enjoy talking to, his parents' house is—for me—just another place I don't belong. Awkward moments are a staple on these visits when we go to say goodbye and his parents hug everyone except me. These goodbyes always end with me squirming out the door as fast as I can while encouraging JJ, Ella, and Nate to hug and kiss Granny and Grandpa goodbye. In the car, Jeff is quietly anxious to get home.

"We were only there three hours, hon," I say.

"Three hours is enough," he responds mechanically.

It's not that Jeff doesn't love his family. He and his mother were extremely close when he was growing up. However, that bond was strained after his sister—the family favorite whose son turned out to be a heroin addict—ended up unmarried and pregnant as a teen. Jeff was sent off to the military and told there was no money for college while his sister, her soon-to-be husband, and new baby (the future addict and favored grandchild) were brought into the family home and catered to. When he returned from boot camp, his mother didn't even go to the airport to pick him up. It was then, he says, that the depression that had plagued him as a child made a reappearance. Later, finally out of the military after a hardship tour in Dessert Storm and a service-connected injury, he spent as much time away from home as possible to avoid living with his sister, her husband, and their toddler.

Jeff's nights, during that time, consisted of drinking and women. I knew this when I married him but wrote it off as a phase. I'd been a partier myself in my college days—Greek life eventually grew on me—and felt bad he'd never had the college experience. It was something his parents provided for his sister at their expense, not once, but twice. With a wounded ego and broken spirit, Jeff eventually moved out of his family home and put himself through college; another thing I admire about him. I didn't notice the drinking. I didn't give the women a second thought. *It was just a phase,* I reasoned. *And who could blame him for wanting to escape with a family like that?*

When Jeff tells me he doesn't know how to be a father, I remind him of his perseverance. I remind him that his sister was handed the world and still asks his parents for monthly mortgage payments. I tell him that he has made his own way and should be proud of all that he has accomplished. He shrugs and tells me he needs a drink, calling himself a failure.

It's easy to blame our parents for the things that go wrong in our adult lives. Quaker Oats spent countless sessions trying to get me to do this, but neither Jeff nor I have found that to be very helpful. Instead, we've tried to find our flaws within ourselves and find ways to grow. I don't believe Roy's abuse or Jeff's mother's indifference had anything to do with why my husband drinks. I also don't blame my parents for the not-so-smart choices I have made. With that said, I do see a duct tape connection between the things we are taught as children and the way we ultimately come to shape our own values. It's something that weighs on me late at night as I struggle to figure out what is best for the kids.

It's funny how you can live in the same house with the same worries and responsibilities and view life so differently. When I began writing this memoir, I started having frequent discussions with Jeff about the way we each perceive our situation. I started asking questions that he was surprisingly candid in answering. I asked things like: "Is alcoholism a disease or a choice?" and "What impact do you think this is having on the kids?" His answers told me that our life experiences and genders made our perception of the situation much different.

"Look at it objectively. Pretend I'm the one who drinks. How would that make you feel as a dad? Like, would you be worried about the kids?" I ask.

"I can't imagine that, hon. I have no way of imagining something that isn't going on. You're the mom and moms don't drink," he replies.

"That's *ridiculous*. You *know* Tyler's mom drinks. That's why she didn't pick him up last week. And so doesn't Libby's mom! How can you say moms don't drink? Beer doesn't care who is opening it!"

He presses his lips to his second-choice Coca Cola. He pauses. "Look, what do you want me to say? Tyler's dad doesn't drink because Tyler's dad is a bum. Maybe his mom drinks because she's stressed out. She's supporting a family. Who cares what other people do?"

"So *that's* what makes it okay to drink? You put food on the table and make money and so that gives you a right to be stressed and drink?" I ask.

"No, but it makes you *want* to drink a hell of a lot more than if you're sitting around all day," he says.

"I work too."

"Yeah. You work too. But you don't feel the pressure that a man feels about making sure the bills are paid and everyone has their cleats and sports shit and art supplies. You don't get what that's like because I always have your back on that stuff," he says.

"I will totally take over the bills. I'll do anything that you need me to do to make it be less pressure on you. You *know* that!"

"What I *know* is that you are freaking out about something that isn't that big of a deal. I don't hit you guys. I don't yell at you guys. I don't do any of that shit. All I want to do when I get home is go in my room and be left alone to drink. Why is that so bad?"

"Don't you think the kids and I need you around so we can be a family?" I retort. I purposely keep my voice low and steady when I ask this. I am fighting back tears now. They would serve no purpose. Reason is what works with Jeff, not pity.

"I don't think the kids care either way. They know who I am and they accept me for it. You're constantly acting like they are going to just start drinking at twelve and fourteen because they know I do it," he says. "That's not going to happen. They aren't my sister's kid."

"Those kids *worship* you. They will do what they see you do. This isn't like you and your dad. They don't hate you like you hated him and they are going to mimic you." I am pleading with him now, hoping something will click.

Conversations like these always have the same result. He walks away feeling attacked and I retreat to the couch defeated. I sit in awe of his ability to reason that as long as he is providing food, clothes, and a roof over the kids' heads he can do whatever he wants to do "in his house". He retreats to the bedroom thinking I'm a controlling monster trying to script what a perfect family life looks like. *If it was only so easy and I had a script to follow.*

***

Robbie got into reading the choose your own adventure series books as a kid. An avid reader with a natural talent for acquiring and retaining knowledge, he could finish several of these books in a mere afternoon. For me, they were aggravating. I'd skip ahead to determine which outcome would be best before making that choice. That is, I wanted to be sure I was able to secure a happy ending before making a decision.

Now, as I face the biggest decision of my life, I crave the pages where I am able to skip ahead. When I look for the best possible outcome, I see our family whole again. I see a marriage that has survived great challenges and a man who has overcome his addiction. And then, there are the worst case outcomes—the ones I am trying so desperately to avoid: The kids being messed up like our nephew from not having a father, not being there to help Jeff get treatment, watching him slowly kill himself. The list goes on. There aren't enough pages in any book to write out all the possible scenarios. *Something tells me Jeff liked choose your own adventure books as a kid. I'll have to ask him. I bet he didn't skip ahead.*

***

Self-diagnosis: Wannabe psychic.

61 Bottles: Mouths of Babes "Verbatim conversations with the kids."

"Do *you* care that he's drinking in front of Chris?" I ask Nathan.

"No. I don't care what a grown up thinks," he says. "I care what my *friends* think. I'd *never* tell them."

JJ is quiet.

Ella is down the road, playing with a friend. I'm glad.

***

Later

"Do your friends ever talk about their parents drinking?" I ask Ella.

"Yeah. Even Tyler's *mom* drinks, Mom!" she responds.

"She does? How does he feel about that?" I ask.

"Well, she doesn't drink like Dad does, Mom. I mean, she only gets wasted on Friday nights. I hate beer."

JJ is quiet.

***

Later

"How do you feel about Dad drinking, J?" I ask.

"I don't know Mom. Dad's just Dad. Whatever."

"But do you want to talk about it?" I press.

"I don't know what to say about it. It's sad," he says.

"Yes, J. It is sad," I sigh.

***

It's Halloween night. Nathan is curled up on the couch after trying to keep his eyes open for a sneak peek of Susan on "Desperate Housewives" in lingerie

I open my laptop to the steady rhythm of Nathan's breathing. The last thing he said to me tonight before falling asleep was, "Do you think they'll show her boobs?" I don't remember how I answered him. I do know that I was sure they'd never show her tits. They don't do that sort of thing on the ABC television station. *God help me on getting through these teenage years.*

The house is warm and its scent is stained with the chili we've enjoyed all weekend. It was spiced medium—not too hot, not too bland, like Goldilocks' favorite meal. My belly is full and I'm staring at my watch, waiting to begin writing for NANOWRIMO, an annual writing challenge to write 50,000 words in only thirty days. Pushing out 1677 words a day isn't difficult for me. I do this every day in my journal. What *is* difficult is making myself stick to it. Like a fad diet, it's easy to get caught up in the early-day hype of good intention and self-improvement promises. But by day ten, cravings for chocolate and a night off from the computer usually get in the way. *What's one piece? My fingers are sore.* Not this time. This year will be different. Now, I have a story to tell.

What makes my story delicious is that I don't know the ending. Normally, I'd find this troublesome. And, as a person living my story, it is. But when I become a character in the story, things change as fast as the seasons in New England. Like the leaves now piling up in my driveway, I'm curious to see where my story will blow if I do nothing but observe it. Instead of pulling out a leaf blower and making sure the lawn is set for winter, I will let Mother Nature take its course and wait to see how my marriage ends up. *Wow. That was less than 400 words. Maybe NANOWRIMO is going to be more difficult than I anticipated.*

I watch Nathan sleep. I know he's sleeping on the couch as an excuse to be near me. A pile up of sleepovers where scary movies like "Scream" and "A Nightmare on Elm Street" were the norm has him panicky over sleeping downstairs. I don't mind it. I like having my baby back. At eleven years old and 120 pounds, he may be a pee wee lineman, but he'll always be my baby.

JJ is growing up quickly too. His size 10.5 adult men's sneakers were carelessly flopped by the front door a few hours ago. They sit next to his father's same sized shoes. Tonight, JJ asked me if he could attend a co-ed sleepover birthday party. I am appalled to think that other parents would allow this. The one girl who will be attending this party is something of a former tomboy but currently

223

wakes up at 4:30 each morning to straighten her hair and apply foundation. I cannot imagine letting Ella do such a thing.

"But *Mom*," he insists. "*Everyone's* going! And it's only *Jen*. It's not like we're going to have a gang bang or something!" *Did I know what a gang bang was at thirteen?*

I ask him if there will be drinking or drugs.

"Jesus, Mom. Not *everyone* drinks." he says.

The kid is right. And if there was ever a kid who hates alcohol it's him. I remind myself this and set back to writing. I produce exactly nine hundred sloppy words, a third of them on the topic of drinking, before closing my laptop and calling it a night.

***

Self-diagnosis: Writer, writing about the one thing that scares her most. So, maybe even brave? Happy Halloween!

60 Bottles: Quaker Oates
"I never liked the texture of that stuff, even the cinnamon kind."

Backing up a little bit, trying to let JJ off the hook, I began seeing a counselor in 2006 about my marriage, issues with depression, and just to get things off my chest. Her name was Joan. A quiet and contemplative woman with Quaker roots, Joan was a good listener who sat with her body facing me while I rambled. Her eyes, not so much. She wasn't great at making eye contact, something that bothered me from the start. Her office was dressed in warm quilts and plants that hung from muted walls. I'd sit, each Tuesday at noon, on her over-stuffed, wine-colored couch and talk about my week.

The first few weeks with Joan were difficult. She seemed more interested in getting a family history than in the things I wanted to talk about, but Jeff had a sign hanging in our master bathroom that read, "The difference between a winner and a loser is that winners never quit." I reminded myself that by going to see Quaker Oates I was working at achieving something—sorting out my life and eventually, coming out on top. I was not a quitter. Unfortunately, neither was he, which was, ironically, our whole problem.

About a month into our sessions together, Quaker Oates stopped me mid-sentence.

"Say that again," she insisted.

"Say what?"

"Say that again. Repeat what you just said."

"I said that Jeff has always been there for me. I said he's a good father. I said he's my best friend and I can talk to him about anything," I repeated.

She nodded. "Are you bullshitting me? Or do you mean that."

I nearly choked on the Poland Springs water I was sipping as it occurred to me that Quaker Oates had just used the word bullshit. I began to like and trust her in that moment; for that moment.

"No. I'm not. I mean, those things are true about him when he's sober," I said.

"So how does that make you feel?"

"What do you mean, how does that make me feel? It feels like crap that he's not that way every day and that he won't stop drinking," I insisted. I dug my toes deeper into my flip flops and waited for her to explain what she was looking for. She remained silent. I was the first one to break that silence.

"Okay. I get it. I mean, if you are saying no one is perfect and I can't expect him to be, that's fine. But don't I have a right to have the guy I married at least be present in the marriage? I mean, can't I expect him to be sober?"

"I think what you can do is worry more about *you* than about what *he* is doing," she said.

I wanted to shove her Alanon-speak up her ass. I went from liking her to despising her in all of about three seconds. *When,* I wondered, *would anyone understand that while it's easy to say 'that's his issue,' it's nearly impossible to live that way?*

You can't just ignore empty beer cans on your counter, can you?

Sessions with Oates continued for about a year. Eventually, I thought of her as Jeff's biggest fan. She smiled huge when I told her about good weekends as a family and frowned when I complained about his drinking. She reminded me, at least once every visit, that not many people could say they were married to their best friend. She told me about how important friendship was and how children did better in a two parent home. I was beginning to think she either had an agenda or was being paid by Jeff.

I returned from sessions with Quaker Oates and shared her views with Jeff. He mimicked her nods and smiles as I recounted her arguments for me to stick with the marriage. Eventually, it was just too much for me. I dropped Joan and never returned to a counselor again. Talking it out, it seemed, wasn't getting me any further than blabbering to Mr. Journal.

I turned toward other women's stories and journeys to find my answers. Gail Haggard had stayed. Hillary had stayed. Hell, there were songs about standing by your man. While every piece of me was screaming, "How could you?" at these women, I was beginning to understand and identify with them. Or, looking back, I was probably just too tired to fight. His drinking didn't feel tangible enough to me: Jeff had never cheated with anything other than the bottle. Other women, or men for that matter, weren't our issue. Beer was his mistress. There was no denying that, none at all. *At least beer isn't skinnier, younger, or prettier than me. In a way, I'd have felt it was easier if he'd had lipstick on his collar. Maybe then, I could leave.*

***

Self-diagnosis: Betrayed wife. Or even the other woman.

59 Bottles: Is All Betrayal the Same?
"Blaming the other woman."

When a man has an affair and is caught, his wife is expected to make a decision. She can leave him or she can stay and work it out, but one thing is almost certain: If the couple decides to work it out, the mistress has to go. That's the standard condition: There will be no phone calls, text messages, or late night meetings with said mistress. No, if the marriage is going to work, that woman is out of their lives. But when your husband's mistress is a blue bottle of alcohol, it gets a little more complicated. Not only was beer Jeff's mistress, but this mistress was something in the very fabric of our home. We couldn't just change rules around, share passwords, or reset our phone numbers. We had to unravel patterns we didn't even fully understand.

He'd taken her to our bed. He'd smelt and sweated of her at night. He'd stored her in our refrigerator. And, he'd even asked me to pick her up on the rare occasion when he hadn't already done it himself. This mistress, this thing, that was playing third wheel in our marriage was not going to be nearly as easy to get rid of as your typical home-wrecker.

Worse, Ms. Beer was a thing Jeff wasn't willing to give up. He would continue to see her every other night and court her on the weekends. While he made good on his promise only to drink at home, he was still absent when he was with her. I desperately wanted someone to understand this.

Quaker Oates hadn't understood. The people at Alanon were so wrapped up in their own issues, combined with rules about crosstalk, that they weren't able to voice their understanding. And my children were frustrated with the entire situation—rightfully wanting to be left out of it. If turning outward for help wasn't going to work, I reasoned, then maybe turning inward—*for real this time*—was the answer.

***

Self-diagnosis: Ready for change. For real, this time.

58 Bottles: All About Me
"Taking back *my* life."

June 1, 2010
I began my journey today. I am really proud of myself. I'm making it all about me. That's right—Mission All About Me. Today, I ate only what my body needed for fuel. I also ordered diet pills that have worked for me in the past. I did a lot of walking and I enjoyed time with Mom today. I was present in the moment and it felt really good. The only thing I did today that I probably shouldn't have was drink a can of soda. But I am okay with that. Know why? Because for today, just for today, I am okay with myself. I have a right to splurge a little. Everything I am reading is about doing it in moderation.

Jeff didn't go to JJ's track meet today. Instead of letting it bother me, I made a conscious choice to eat a salad, rather than the chicken alfredo that was in the fridge for supper. I feel good about that. And, better yet, I decided I can't be responsible for his actions and I didn't even let it get me in a bad mood. I'm sure these things would sound like no big deal to other people. But you, Mr Journal, know how big this is for me.

June 4, 2010
I've lost exactly no pounds since beginning this new diet thing three days ago. It's frustrating to say the least. I know. It's comical. I know this takes

time, but still. I just need something to change quickly; something to come easy.

Jeff's drunk as usual and I'm sitting here trying to ignore it. My stomach is growling. I'm trying to compare our addictions in my mind. Maybe, I've decided, if I can understand my addiction to food, I can understand his to alcohol. Maybe that will make the almighty blue can slam seem more logical and forgivable. Forgiving and being able to accept his drinking would be so much easier than doing anything real about it. I'm good at taking the easy way out, but I'm tired of living that way.

Tonight, when the sun has gone down and no one can see my fat ass doing it, I'm going to go for a bike ride. I don't want the kids to come with me. I want to do this alone. I feel alone and I need to fix this alone. If I can fix me, maybe I can then work at fixing my life. How can I make decisions about my life until I am in a place to make a logical choice? Right now, I'm just a mess. I need to mop up that mess and stop hating myself. Then, and only then, can I fix the rest.

***

Self-diagnosis: Determined.

57 Bottles: Refocusing Self
"Making a new kind of list."

If there's one message you get in Alanon it's that you can't take responsibility for your loved one's drinking. You can't blame yourself for their behaviors and you can't let their drinking get to you. *Much, much easier said than done. Who came up with this shit?* Instead, to be the healthiest you can, you should try to ignore the drinker's patterns and fill your time with the things that make your heart sing. Simple, right?

Wrong.

If alcoholism is a disease—and I'm not so sure I buy that, it seems like a person makes a choice whether or not to pick up the bottle—then it's a contagious disease. Actually, when I think about it, alcoholism reminds me of conjunctivitis. Or maybe head lice. It affects the entire family and everyone in the alcoholic's life. It makes sense that many of the people I've met in support groups suffer from depression—another of alcoholism's partners in crime.

I've had issues with depression since my early twenties. It was somewhere around the middle of 2009 that eight years of living with Jeff's drinking began to get to me. I looked in the mirror one day and didn't recognize myself. I'd packed on more than fifty pounds, felt very little reason to get out of bed in the morning, and found myself getting winded after doing the smallest of household chores. I'm surprised I didn't have big green boogers falling out of my eyes and tiny bugs lay-ing eggs in my hair.

A year later, after being laid off from my job at a mental health agency, I was in even worse shape—nearly ninety pounds overweight and contemplating suicide. Head lice would have been a welcome distraction. I decided I needed to do something. I needed to make a decision and I needed to start living for me. It was in March of 2010 that I began writing this book. I promised myself it would be an honest portrait of my life and marriage, for better or for worse.

I knew the Alanon meeting folks could not save me. I knew that doing things the way I was doing them—chain smoking and spending my days in a reality television coma on the couch—wasn't working. What I didn't know, any longer, was myself.

Something instinctual told me that the best way to pull myself out of this was to dig out my love for life. Nick-named 'Sunshine' by Farmer Charm-ing, I had a reputation of being the smiley, happy person in the family. I was always the one who made things fun and, as Jeff put it, "made the house a home". I couldn't remember the last time I'd smiled. I wanted to smile again. I began my journey of recovery by writing a list of things I en-joyed.

March 13, 2010
I don't know who I am anymore. I'm a fat old lady. I'm unhealthy. I don't even recognize myself. I want to be so much more than this. I watch the

"Biggest Loser" and I want to cry. I know I can be more and I can do more but I don't know where to begin. All I can think to do is to start by trying to be my own best friend. I can't remember where I heard that before, but it makes sense.

I need to stop relying on Jeff to tell me what sort of mood to be in. I'm numb. But letting an alcoholic grouch define my moods is worse than being numb. I need to find a way to wake up each day with something to look forward to. Secretly, I'm so glad I am not working right now. If I was working, I'd be in big trouble. I don't even understand how I used to get up and go to work everyday. I can hardly shower these days. I haven't had a shower yet today and it's already time to cook supper. At least I haven't stopped doing that. Thank God for the kids. Please, let me find a way to prevent this from happening to Ella...

What makes me happy?

When the kids smile. *There's got to be a way to make that happen more.*

Getting my nails done. *I can make an appointment this week.*

Shopping. *Who are you kidding? That's just another addiction. No different than smoking.*

Reading. *I just finished the* Twilight *series. To-morrow I will go get another one I've been hoping to read,* Eat, Pray, Love. *It sounds like her story is similar in some ways. Maybe I can get some inspiration from that?*

Writing. That's a no-brainer. I need to just keep keeping at it. I finally got an acceptance letter for two of my poems to be put in an anthology. That's a really big deal. I should be celebrating. Maybe I could print out the acceptance letter and hang it on the wall. I have read that many writers hang all their rejection slips up. I can't imagine doing that. Who needs that kind of negative reinforcement?

Back to the writing, I need to be doing it every day. And I need to be helping people. I can combine those two things. I can write about my story and maybe help someone else with it. I know that I feel alone. Maybe sharing my words and experience would be of some help to someone else? I can't imagine how Jeff would feel about that, but I can't keep living based on his reactions. Remember?

Nature. I spent the day inside. It's spring and I should be out there. Instead, I'm inside. I'm afraid for people to see me at this weight—242.5 lbs. I am just mortified at how I look.

Feeling good about myself physically. The only way to fix this is to start using that stupid treadmill I bought with such high hopes. I will start doing that tonight. Maybe if I do it for a half hour each day it will make a difference? I don't know, but it can't hurt. Well, my quads: It could definitely hurt my quads.

***

Self-diagnosis: Seeking authentic happiness. Ready to do something about it for once.

236

56 Bottles: Letting It Get to Me
"If at first you don't succeed."

Who cares what day it is? Nothing changes…
Dear Mr. J,
So much for Mission All About Me. I've failed. Again. Time for a pity party. No. I'm not doing that. I'm not letting it get to me. Not again.

He called me Sunshine again today. I certainly don't feel like the sun. But, oh, how I want to be. I wonder what he would think if he really knew what I was thinking about these days. I wonder how he doesn't get the hint from my clothes. I don't think I've worn anything but black in months. Suicide, suicide, suicide. Do you think it's contagious? He talks about doing it so much that I'm thinking maybe he's got the right idea. Maybe he's on to something? Maybe God has a better plan for us— only I'm the one who needs the dirt nap? Hmm.

Either way, true to form, here's a bright and happy little spin on where I'm at these days. Sorry it's been so long since I've written. It takes time to boot up the optimism card these days…

The Bright Side of Suicide

Being suicidal isn't so bad.
I no longer worry about material possessions. Why the need? Instead, I create lists. Who will want my striped socks—the kind that go right up to your knees? Whom should I leave the dirty dishes

237

to? Ha! My third grade teacher, who always hated me. Maybe I'll have fried eggs—burnt—for dinner tonight. Good luck with the pan.

I make lists of others who have gone before, silently giving nods to Sylvia Plath—wondering how she managed to keep her head in that stove. Terry Kath played Russian roulette. (I always bet on black.) And then there was Virginia. I wonder, were the voices just too bad?

You don't need a job when you're suicidal. And being laid off, laid up, or just plain worried about getting laid are perfectly fine states of mind when there is no tomorrow. My boss was a prick who demanded loyalty but wound up firing me because it'd be easier on the numbers. I broke my foot climbing the maple tree, wondering if the rope was strong enough. And I haven't had sex in years. (Okay, not really, but it sounds good!)

Naw. Being suicidal isn't so bad.

Your priorities change when you know you'll never see another summer. So much for spring cleaning. Window dust and moldy ceilings add a certain rustic charm. Should I clean out the cupboards before I pick up another xanax prescription? Will three bottles be enough? What should I do with my old love letters? Tonight I'll build a bonfire.

I get to exact revenge, now that I am suicidal. I wasn't good enough? I wasn't strong enough? My heart wasn't in it? Don't worry about it, me, or the color of the roses you carry to my headstone. I will be just fine. But you? You will live with guilt for all of time. The apple doesn't fall far from the tree, they say.

I don't sleep now that I have a plan. There will be plenty of time for sleep. And now, I am able to stay up with the crickets. I keep the man selling cookers and fast chops company late into the night. I look at his dead eyes—mirrors to my own, and wonder, doesn't he know? Hasn't he heard?

Being suicidal isn't so bad.

See? I can be suicidal too: Just like you.

***

Years later, we're watching Nathan's football team get trampled by a rival city when Mom announces that she and Dad want to be cremated. I try not to seem surprised by this sudden announcement, which happens to be on the cusp of Dad's next-day stress test for a bad heart.

"Um, okay. And why is that?" I ask, keeping my eyes on the field. "Nice hit, Nathan!"

"Nana is worried no one will visit her grave when she dies," she replies, popping a handful of popcorn into her mouth.

"Okay. Why is that?"

"She says that no one will have any reason to go to Pennsylvania because Grampy's already dead and the only time we visit Grampy is when we go to visit her," she says, sipping her diet Pepsi.

"So that means you and Dad want to be cremated?"

"Yes. Right, hon?" she asks, nudging my father.

Dad, who seems more focused on the football players creating a fuss in the stands than the ones on the field, looks to her for an explanation. After Mom explains that, "Lisa wants to know why we want to be cremated," he nods his head.

"Yep."

"Okay," I bite. "I'll keep that in mind. Is someone dying that I'm not aware of?"

Mom laughs, telling me that funerals are expensive and totally unnecessary.

"What if no one came?" She looks horrified. It's as if her entire existence would be determined by pure numbers. Like a mathematical equation, a person's net worth comes down to the number of people who attend one's funeral.

"So? The people you'd care about would be there," I shrug.

"I think that would be just horrible! Imagine if no one came?"

"Well, Ma, if you are going to be cremated then that's not something you will have to worry about. Do you know what you want done with the ashes? I mean, I don't think you want to be stuck in a box do you?"

She looks at me, as if she's never considered this before and turns to my father. "In the backyard?"

He nods.

Why is this a team decision? I wonder. *It's at the death part that you* get *to part.*

"Okay. It's settled then," she exclaims, like she's just found the prize at the bottom of her Applejacks. "Scatter us in the backyard."

We sit in silence while the opposing team scores. The silence is interrupted only by her final comment: "If someone else owns the house, make sure you sneak in the backyard and scatter the ashes while they are at work, okay?"

I stare at her. *Who is this person?* "Okay, Ma. We'll sneak in there in the dark wearing black hoods and stuff. It'll be a real covert operation. What's your *deal*?"

Now, I can't stop thinking about my *own* funeral. I've instructed Jeff and my now-morbid mother that I require two very important last wishes: 1. That I am also cremated because I refuse to be trapped in a tiny box, and 2. That I'm cremated with my inhaler, while wearing socks. Clothing is optional. Nothing tight, please.

"Why the hell do you need socks?" Jeff asks, his frown turning into an amused curl.

"You know how I hate having cold feet."

"Hon, you are going to be cremated. I don't think you need to worry too much about being cold," he reasons.

"I don't care. I need my inhaler so I can breathe and I need socks so my feet aren't cold."

"Whatever you want, hon. Just dump my ass in a dumpster and spit on me. Oh, and throw in a beer," he laughs.

***

Self-diagnosis: Not remotely suicidal, but concerned that, maybe, I should be. (At least people would know what to do with me.)

55 Bottles: Shine On!
"Bring on the happiness, dammit."

"Kids," I called, waking unusually early one morning. "Don't go anywhere after school today. Come straight home. We're having a party."

"A party for what?" Nate asked.

"I'm tired of everyone being sad around here. We're having a Happiness Party."

"What's a Happiness Party, Mom?" Ella looked at me like I'd gone officially mad. She eyed me from behind her thick lashes—so thick she sometimes appeared to be blinking in slow motion. I'd always wanted eyelashes like those.

"You'll see. Just be sure to come right home, okay?"

I spent the day preparing for the party. I started at the dollar store, gathering up all the yellow smiley face balloons and paper cups and plates I could hold. I bought bottles of spray silly string, party favors, and yellow poster board. I went to the market and picked up ingredients for a special dinner, as well as a happiness cake which I promptly set home to make.

By the time everyone arrived home, the house was transformed into a yellow sea of smiley faces and confetti.

"What's going on, hon?" Jeff asked, when he returned from work.

I told him my plan. He smiled. "That's my Sunshine."

We spent that April evening spraying each other with crazy spray in the back yard, eating cake, and decorating the poster board with pictures of us happy and smiling. We made posters and other signs of things that made us each, as individuals, happy. Jeff's had a sports car, a barn for animals, a cross, and a picture of the family on it.

"Aren't you going to put beer there?" Nate asked, innocently.

"No. I don't need beer there," Jeff said, looking at the table. "I'm happy right now."

***

Self-diagnosis: Ordinary mother and wife with an everyday dream. Maybe even good at it, sometimes.

54 Bottles: Dreams
"A conversation with my soul."

"What do you dream about?"

Dreams? Easy. I dream about the book. I dream about what I will write and how I will write it. In my sleep, I dream about ways to convey the whole truth about my family—not just about Jeff's drinking. While his drinking is a big part of our lives, I wouldn't say it defines us. There's so much more to us than that. I mean, we laugh together, we love one another. Things like that.

"And what are your dreams for the future?"

I guess I want to find a way for all of us to be happy. I want him to want to live. I want my best friend back. I dream of a day where we can all be healthy. I don't just mean physically healthy. I mean emotionally healthy. I dream of a day where my husband and I don't insist on hurting ourselves.

Specifically? I dream of Thanksgivings.

"Thanksgivings?"

Yes. I dream of Thanksgivings, years from now, when the kids are much older and have children of their own. I dream of spoiling the grandchildren and Jeff taking the kids out to the barn to feed and pet the animals. Jeff doesn't drink in these dreams. He's like Grampy and has quit, not for the sake of those grandchildren, but for himself. He is at peace and happy. I watch from the kitchen window, knowing I made the right decision in staying with him.

"And do dreams come true?"

99 Bottles

ERIN LEE

Absolutely.

***

Self-diagnosis: Believer.

53 Bottles: Me & Mr. J
"Dying on the inside."

May 19, 2010

JJ has a track meet after school today. Mom is coming down to do lunch and go with me to the meet. This morning, after texting me to pick up a certified letter at the post office for him, I texted Jeff the schedule. Texting this way is more common for us these days because I don't want to get bitchy with him by talking. I'm glad I stuck with texting this morning. I told him about the time of the track meet, that Nathan would be staying at Tyler's house to play with him until about seven, and that JJ and I would be home (possibly with Mom) at around seven too. I was totally shocked, which is really dumb, when he responded, "Okay, hon. I'll be home by two and drunk by 2:30." I texted back, "Are you serious?" He never responded.

It's possible he just reached work and never got my final text. But I doubt that. I am sure he thinks it is quite reasonable that he, the only breadwinner and, apparently, the only one who feels stress in this lifetime, should be drunk by 2:30 in the afternoon. I'm not sure what part of "only breadwinner" is complicated for him. I can't imagine that his boss is going to be all that happy to learn he left the office for the day by two. And he certainly can't take work calls slurring...

Alcoholism is not only progressive, it is terminal. I am starting to believe this really will kill him. It makes me so angry. The kids deserve better than this. Whether we are with him or not, he has an obligation to be their father. That obligation is emotional, as well as financial. But, most important to me, it's emotional. I was watching Intervention *last night and the woman was an alcoholic. Her father was blaming himself for her alcoholism because she'd grown up in a home where there was alcohol abuse. I don't feel bad for the father. I think he should feel badly for drinking around his children. Children deserve better than that. I can't imagine what all this feels like for them.*

When we had the kids, I wanted only what was best for them. I wanted to give them the world. Jeff and I had very little material things, but we had love. We had lots of love. I thought, that with love, we could do anything. I thought that we were invincible because there was nothing greater than the sum of us. I thought that we could handle any obstacle and any situation and come out of it loving each other. I still love Jeff and I always will. Our bond is thick. Much of that bond, though, was built on bad experiences. This drinking thing is no different.

It's going to be really hard for me to print 99 Bottles, *if I ever do. There is a part of me that feels so disloyal for putting it all out there. But I also know that I've looked everywhere for personal stories with intimate details of the journey of living with an alcoholic. There are so few of them. There is so little out there on what it's really like to live with an alcoholic and how it destroys families. I know I needed something to read that would make me know I was not alone. So, for that reason, I feel*

247

compelled to keep writing it every day. Even if it's just a little bit.

I'm still shell-shocked to know I can't bring Mom home after track today, even if I wanted to. He will be drunk and that would be mortifying. Maybe I should bring her. Maybe if he was embarrassed it would snap him out of it. Who am I kidding? He'd probably just lash out at her and I'd be the one embarrassed. And why, exactly, isn't he coming to the meet?

Suicide seems like the only escape sometimes. Between the weight gain, not having a job, and this depression that I can't seem to shake, I don't know where to go with any of this. Getting divorced makes me feel like a failure. I can't imagine any other man wanting me. I had my chances with other men. Over and over, I chose Jeff. I am not sure why. Maybe it was love. Maybe it was "the right thing to do". Or maybe it was for the kids. But, these days, I'm beginning to realize, it wasn't the choice for me. Or, maybe, it was and I just can't face it.

I spend my nights alone. I sleep on the couch because I can't stand being in the same bed with his stinky sweat and drunken ramblings. He's told me a million times he'd try to cut down. But these days, instead of making more false promises, he says things more like, "I'll never stop drinking" and, "Our life's not going to change, so don't think I am." I'm tired of these statements. It's not because they are defeatist. It's because I know they are his reality. And, I don't like where that leaves me. It leaves me with the reality that I have a choice to make. It's a choice I've put off making for way too long because I am a coward. At the same time, I feel if I don't make one it will be terminal not only for him, but also for me.

***

Self-diagnosis: Angry and resentful weakling.

52 Bottles: Priorities
"Checking the kids for damage."

My Husband

Dulls the heartburn that comes with supporting a family
my husband   hardworking with calloused hands   his head under
the kitchen sink, mucking out the grease I poured in it last night
but won't fess up to   the boy who grew up military brat
with two pairs of bellbottoms to his name   a Dallas Cowboys' blanket
father of two sons   one daughter and creases in his forehead
Mimicking the scowl he wears   a tie pulled taunt around his neck
when he returns from his eight to six rendezvous with the corporate world
and races toward the fridge   graceful as an eagle on the soccer field
reliving a dream he forgot to fall asleep to so long ago   "great kick, hon."
to the youngest girl, who spins in circles picking daisies as bigger boys
blast headers   gentle-voiced and the first to run out on the field for injuries
and the little boy who gets nose bleeds   took LSD in high school

*and threatens to kill our own should they ever do
the same   love*

*laughing at my clumsy quirks that land me in a
cast   helping me limp*

*to the car   days   nights in the ER   first to
help the lady*

*on the side of the road   a spare gas tank
spare change   clothes*

*that are the last to be replaced   (I wear a new
bra   kids need cleats)*

*skinny-legged six foot plus   mocha eyes to hide
the pain   paydays*

*never fast enough   took another sip   ears numb
on need   took a Tums one night*

and drank himself to sleep.

***

Escape, happiness parties and false starts at self-improvement missions are wonderful fantasies in their own ways and, likely, a natural part of the process when you are in the midst of a deep depression. But it can't always be quick fixes when you have children to raise. On Mother's Day, that year of my millionth failed mission, I was jolted into reality when Nathan said to me, "Mom, we don't see you very much anymore. Can we spend the day together?" (Enter tremendous guilt.)

When I look back at my life, I see my kids as my greatest accomplishment. I often wonder how I got the three most perfect children on the planet. Perhaps it was that bingo card that gave me the good luck of striking the jackpot. I have a hard time thinking it was anything but blind luck. I often sigh, telling myself that they couldn't, and wouldn't, possibly be this good if it had anything to do with the person I am. Other times, I tell myself I'm underestimating myself—that I'm a good mother. I know both are true. *Only, a good mother would have left.*

Watching videos of my tenth birthday party, I am struck when I see my brother Mark on my lap. I am patiently and encouragingly allowing him to open each and every one of my presents. I'm virtually ignoring the friends—telling them it's my baby brother's job to open the presents, blow out the candles, etc. I'm informing them they need to wait; we *will* go out to play later. It was more important to me that my little brother enjoy my day than any of us. *No* wonder *I didn't have any friends.* It was on Mark that I learned how to be a mother.

JJ is a straight-'A' student and stellar athlete. He dribbles down the soccer field as gracefully as he calculates math equations in his head. Nathan is an honors student who has no fear on a football field and leads his lacrosse teams to victories again and again. Ella is a talented artist who somehow inherited an ability to sing. Watching her in school plays is a joy. All the kids are confident, secure, relatively happy, and balanced. They are healthy and socially accepted. Somehow, I even managed to raise popular kids. But popular these days is not what popular was in the 80s. Most certainly, it's not what I always thought it would be.

I've learned, even popular kids have their problems. Still, I'm often struck by the confidence JJ,

Ella and Nate exhibit when it comes to peer pressure. Things like "Mom, who *cares* what they think?" and, "I don't mind if you chaperone my field trip. I'd like it," or, "Will you coach me in soccer?" never fail to surprise me. When I was young, the last place on earth I wanted either of my parents to be was close to my socially inept geek squad handful of friends. *No way, Jose!* The last thing I needed was for my ammo-packed peers to have more slurs against me.

Despite being so well-adjusted, I often worry how the kids will turn out in the end. I worry about how my former need to discuss pretty much every emotion I had has affected JJ in particular. I guess what I'm saying is I don't want them to grow up to be me. Or their father. I worry about this constantly. They laugh and call me crazy.

***

Quaker Oates-generated diagnosis: Generalized anxiety disorder. Always worried about everything and anything.

51 Bottles: A Child's Perspective
"I'm never going to drink, Mom."

"I'm never going to drink," JJ proclaims out of the blue.

"Well, that's a good thing! But there is such a thing as drinking responsibly, you know," I say. "Not everyone drinks as much as Dad."

"I don't care. I hate it."

"I hate it too," Ella says.

Nathan is listening from the backseat of my Jeep wrangler, the one Jeff presented me on our tenth anniversary after promising to buy it a few years prior. Aside from alcohol consumption, Farmer Charming always keeps his promises. I could count on that like I could count the beers on my counter.

"I hate it too. But I know I will do it someday," Nate says, finally joining his siblings. Nathan's always been the most honest of the children.

"Really? Why?" I ask, trying not to panic.

"Kids drink in college. Look at Uncle Jack," he tells me.

"Yes, kids drink in college. But not until they are twenty-one. And they *never* drink and drive," I say, hearing my mother in my voice.

"I know, Mom," he says.

"Dude, you're a dumbass. Why would you want to drink at all. Look at Dad. And what a waste of money," JJ scolds.

"Uncle Jack's lame," Ella says, looking to JJ for approval.

"I don't care about money," Nate says.

I sigh, pulling into the library parking lot. The kids are out of the car before I know how to end the conversation. *Are they going to be okay?* I wonder. *Jesus. What has he done? What have I done by staying? This isn't even close to all about me anymore.*

***

Self-diagnosis: Guilty. Shit mother.

50 Bottles: This Ain't Disneyland, Folks
"A family vacation is a countdown to Dad's rage."

I was thirteen the first time my parents took us to Disney World. Pimply, unpopular, and awkward in my own skin, I was more than happy to take some time off from school to go somewhere else—anywhere else.

"You're gonna love it, Lisa. It's so much better than anything you've ever seen. The rides are better. The place is *huge*," Mom promised, as she cheerfully packed our suitcases with new clothes specifically for our trip. "Here, fold this. I want to make sure everything is just perfect."

I walked around Disney wearing a Goofy hat. Goofy's long ears fell perfectly over the sides of my face like blinders on a horse. Robbie and I jumped from one line to the next with my parents and Mark in tow. From Pirates of the Caribbean first thing in the morning to Space Mountain after nightfall, the trip was go, go, go. We didn't want to miss a thing. While no one can do every ride and see every attraction in Disney in a week, we certainly gave it our best shot.

Mom cried looking up at the gigantic Epcot ball on the last night of our trip. I understood her not wanting to leave this magical place and reached to rub her back. She hugged me.

"I'm okay," she said, watching the fireworks sail over our heads to light up the ball.

"But why are you crying?"

"I just don't want to go home," she said.

Years later, Mom would remind me that our house had been under construction for over a year at the time of that trip. Sick of tripping over plywood and random hand tools, the last place she wanted to be was at the house. As an adult, that finally made sense.

My family returned to Disney a few years later. This time, there were no Goofy ears and I was more worried about the teenage boys at Typhoon Lagoon than I was about getting in line for Space Mountain with Robbie. I was staring at one of those boys at Typhoon Lagoon when I stubbed my toe on a fake ledge.

"Damn!" I screamed, no longer caring who was looking at me in my rainbow bikini.

My father turned back to me.

"You okay, hon?"

The big toe on my left foot was blowing up fast. I suspected it was broken. The nurse at the Typhoon Lagoon infirmary confirmed it was broken, telling us we could go to the hospital but that there was really nothing anyone could do for a broken toe but tape it. I spent the rest of that Disney trip in a wheelchair, cutting lines because of my temporarily disabled status, and no longer worried about boys.

Mom didn't cry when we left this time. And I didn't return to Disney for twenty years. By the time I did return, it was me who was the mother. It was my turn to cry.

***

Jeff was working as a director for a homecare nursing facility when he came home one day and announced that his company was celebrating it's 35th anniversary the following year in Disney World. This would be our chance to take the kids to Disney without the expenses of a hotel room and other perks that the company would foot the bill for. I was ecstatic. The kids were thrilled. Jeff reached for a beer.

"How come you aren't excited about this?" I asked, later that night. Jeff had been to Disney as a kid and loved it. I couldn't understand why he wouldn't want to go back.

"Hon, are you serious? You don't see why I wouldn't want to go?" He stared at me like I was an alien he didn't recognize.

"Well, no. Why *wouldn't* you want to go?"

"It's for fucking work! Are you kidding me? If your work was going to have a big party in Disney would you want to go?"

"For free? Hell yes!"

"Not for free, Lisa! Not for free! They cover the hotel. They don't cover airfare, food, tickets into the parks. This shit is going to cost us five *grand*."

I rolled my eyes. "No *way* is it going to be *that* expensive! What other chance have we got to take them where we won't have to pay for a hotel?"

"I'm not saying we can't go. I just told the kids we were going. I'm saying that you guys should go, have fun, and enjoy it. I'll be working. And I don't want to think or talk about this for the next year," he said. "It's a great opportunity for you and the kids, but just know that the last thing in the world I want to do is pay that kind of money to go somewhere to hang out with people from work."

Jeff's attitude toward the trip didn't change as we neared closer to our departure date. The kids and I could no longer contain our excitement a week before the trip. We talked about our plans, watched videos of the parks online, and made attempts to include Jeff by finding things we could do with him after working hours. He did his best to nod his head and offered us forced smiles.

We stayed at the Buena Vista Palace in Downtown Disney. The hotel was four stars, offering balconies and generous sized beds. There was a swimming pool, a hot tub, a local wild crane who was very people friendly, palm trees, and an arcade. *Yes, this place would do.* I tried my best to keep a cheerful smile and ignore Jeff's cynical comments about his next day agenda. He managed to have fun after I promised not to give him crap about his drinking while we were on the trip.

The kids and I were experts at the parks by the time we finally arrived at Magic Kingdom. Our research had paid off and, despite March being the park's busy season, we managed to get on all the rides we'd listed as our "must do's". JJ was in charge of park maps and navigating us through crowds and Ella was in charge of bussing and transportation to and from the parks. They behaved like angels and we had a hell of a time.

At night, we'd return to the room and tell Jeff about the day's activities. One night, we ordered room service and ate together. Each night, Jeff drank. And as promised, I didn't say a word about it. Later, he told me that each of those nights he'd go out on the balcony after we went to sleep and consider jumping off our thirteenth floor slab. I was glad he spared me from that information while we were on the trip. But, still, I could not ignore that things had gone too far. I just kept my mouth shut. There was no reason to ruin the trip.

We managed to get more time with Jeff toward the end of the week, sharing a fabulous day together at Disney's Animal Kingdom. We made Jeff's love for animals and interest in going on a safari top priorities of the day. His eyes shined like they hadn't in years as we took an hour long safari through the park's extensive land. He clicked off shot after shot of rhinoceroses, elephants, lions, and kangaroos with my camera. And while he watched the animals, I watched him—thrilled to have my Farmer Charming back. He didn't drink for the rest of the trip.

No one saw me cry when we left Disney $5,201 lighter. I thought of my mother. But mostly, I thought of Jeff. Seeing him so happy made it difficult to board a plane I knew was taking us right back to the very stressors that caused him to drink and made him so unhappy. I made a mental note to remember the look in his eyes that day so I could find a way to help him find it again. I told myself that if I ever saw that look again, on a regular basis, I'd know it'd all been worth it.

Even Disney World doesn't fix a family suffering from substance abuse issues. Only a week later, I still felt like I was on Space Mountain, joggling back and forth between the highs and lows of my life and Jeff's drinking schedule. The only difference now was that I was no longer riding in the dark. I was more than comfortable with the twists and turns our family would encounter from day to day. And somehow, I was beginning to feel less motion sickness these days.

***

Self-diagnosis: Conditioned.

49 Bottles: Two Roads
"Nana's starfish."

A hack New England poet, I'm all too familiar with Robert Frost's *Road Less Traveled.* Frankly, I find the poem a little aggravating. This is probably because it challenges us to do something unexpected and unconventional. I've never been comfortable with going too far outside my comfort zone—but have always craved just that. I've always admired those who take the road less traveled. But I wonder sometimes if it is more difficult to take that new road when the people you love and admire most have always taken the paved one. It's never easy to be the first. Yet, somehow, I usually am.

My grandmother, Eloise, is someone I have always adored. She is kind and gentle and energetic. She was faithful to Grampy despite years of beatings while he was an active alcoholic. I'd looked up to my grandmother for that for years. Nana was a non-drinker until Grampy died. She began drinking socially after he died, stating that she could "finally have a nice glass of wine in the house."

Spending time with Nana was always fun for me. She out-shopped Mom and I for the majority of my life—running through stores like a thirty-something. Even in her 80s, Nana has the same taste as me. My mother, a conservative person, calls our taste "tacky." We call it bright, cheerful, and eclectic.

Grampy was a hardworking man. He drank, Mom claimed, because of the stresses of supporting five children with only a sixth grade education. He drank to the point of excess on long binges twice a year—beginning on Memorial day, through my mother's July birthdays, and during the holidays. So, for my mother, her birthday and Christmas were nothing to look forward to during her childhood. As her version goes, when my mother discovered she was pregnant with me, she went to Grampy and told her that if he wanted to be in his first grandchild's life, he needed to get sober. He stopped drinking in February of 1974 and never took another sip. He never hit Nana or my mother or her sisters or her brother again. And I never saw him take a sip.

I loved Grampy dearly and never held his past behaviors against him. My brother, Mark, resented him until the day he died for the way he treated my mother. Grampy died of lung cancer at the age of seventy-six in 2007. He spent the last thirty-two years of his life trying to make up for the way he'd treated Nana during the first twenty of their lives together but I suspect she never forgave him completely. She definitely never forgot.

I wonder, sometimes, if my grandmother is glad she chose the road she did. She was able to get over thirty years of sobriety and love out of my grandfather once he stopped drinking. But, was it too late for her to forgive? I recently visited her. She spoke fondly of Grampy and never once mentioned the drinking years. Instead, she talked about a starfish he'd found for her on a beach in Aruba. It was leaning up against a window in the breezeway of the home he'd built for her so many years ago— the very room he died in with Nana and Aunt Martha at his side. I closed my eyes and pictured a sober Jeff finding me such a starfish someday.

I wrote the following "This I Believe" essay in my journal following that trip to Nana's house in 2009:

I Believe in Nana's Choice (Even though I'm not sure she does herself)

I schedule my life around twelve-packs of Labatt Blue beer. Drinking nights, hiding car keys, dodging insults, and shielding the children are my rituals. Scarlet creeps upon my cheeks at the town recycling plant as I empty the bottles on Saturdays. Oddly enough, I'm a non-drinker.

Sure, I drank back in college. I attended regular fraternity parties and even "forced" myself to take the obligatory Sunday night off from binge drinking. But all of that ended with college. I had dreams of becoming a successful journalist and marrying my Farmer Charming. Beer was not part of those dreams.

I've been married to an alcoholic for seven years. He was not a big drinker when I met him. For seven years, I have hid his beer cans from the children, made excuses for his sometimes wild behavior—such as riding his bicycle in the middle of a winter storm down to the convenience store with a backpack to get one more forty ounce bottle— and accepted the fact that he won't eat dinner with the family on drinking nights because food absorbs alcohol. Counting beer cans on the counter, carrying two hundred pounds of dead weight to bed, watching him urinate in the middle of the hallway, cleaning it up, and gritting my teeth through drunken ramblings have become habits for me.

I have thought about leaving many times. I have even dreamt of a new Prince Charming rescuing my children and I, but I have talked myself out of it. Those who say it takes more courage to leave haven't heard the stories of the women in Alanon who recall watching their kids get into cars with their intoxicated ex-husbands because it's their visiting day. They have no idea what it takes to muster the courage to hang in there "one day at a time".

My widowed grandmother was married to an alcoholic for more than fifty years. Once, he threw a frozen turkey at my grandmother. Recently, she and I spent the day together. I wanted to ask her if it had been worth staying with my grandfather all those years. I looked at the widowed wedding band she still wore and almost brought it up. I wondered if I would ever wear a wedding band as a widow. Something stopped me. Whatever her answer was, I decided, it didn't matter. She had made her choice and I respected it.

I believe in loyalty, commitment, and stability. I believe in for better or for worse marriage vows and an obligation to give my children a two-parent home. I believe in forgiveness and the power of healing. I believe I am doing the right thing. I be-

lieve in Nana's choice and that, sometimes, it takes more strength to stay than it does to leave.

***

My original draft for the "This I Believe" project essay was much longer. It was over 2500 words, to be precise. But it is there, in the above five hundred words, that I can nutshell my decisions up until that point when it came my marriage. That is, when you get married, it's supposed to be for good times and for bad. All marriages have their ups and downs. However, I'm not so sure that most peoples' bad times are quite like ours. I've wondered, have other women seen lightning bolts come out of their husband's usually gentle eyes when asked to put the beer away?

This wondering got the best of me in 2010 when I decided to brave the answers to my questions. Clinically depressed, the heaviest I'd ever been, unemployed, and desperate to piece together my life, I asked my mother the question I'd been dying to ask Nana all those years. Grampy had been dead for about three years by now and I was convinced now was the time to get the answers I deserved. I wanted to know, for once, the truth in my family's history with alcohol.

"Do you think Nana is glad she stuck it out with Grampy after all those years of drinking, even after he quit?" I fixed my eyes on my mother's face. We sat across from one another during one of our monthly lunchtime girl dates. She looked down at her chicken lime fiesta dish and inhaled. She looked back up, looking me directly in the eye. Her head moved from left to right, slowly.

"No, I don't think she was," she sighed. "I think they were really different people and that things were different back then. It makes me sad, he loved her very much."

I wasn't able to finish the rest of my own chicken—a rarity for me—upon hearing her answer.

"But how can you really know that?" I prodded.

"I don't think she ever forgave him," Mom conceded, as if she'd thought about this a million times before but had never voiced it out loud.

"Oh."

I had a similar conversation with Aunt Martha (who still has the cleanest refrigerator in America) about six months later. It was Aunt Martha who informed me that Grampy had quit drinking after a lot more than Mom's pleas for her daughter to have a sober grandfather. Grampy, Martha told me, had hit rock bottom, hard, before volunteering to go to treatment. The timing of my birth, she insisted, was pure coincidence. Family cycles carry on and all stories are open to both interpretation and misinformation, the way a person wants to tell it, I learned.

"Daddy was laying in the street somewhere and had lost all control of his body before they called Mommy," she said, her voice strong and matter of fact over the phone. "He told Mommy he'd go to treatment only if they could get him in that night. So Mommy called Father Pete and Father Pete found a way to get him in the VA hospital that night. There was a long waiting list but Mommy was close to the church and Father did her a favor."

"I had no idea," I told her, explaining my mother's habit of censoring the rougher parts of the truth to her children. "That's good for me to know. Thank you for telling me. I always thought he just decided to stop one day."

"No. There was a lot more to it than that. I remember times when he didn't come home for days because he was always at the bar," she recalled.

For us, it's different. Jeff never leaves. Then, I asked the inevitable: "Do you think Nana is glad she stayed with Grampy all those years because he was able to finally quit?"

Her answer shouldn't have surprised me. If rated PG Mom had told me the R version of the family history, how could I have expected Aunt Martha, who lived a much more open and modern lifestyle to have ever answered any different. Her voice was a solid XXX.

"No, Lisa."

"But she misses him. I know she does." I was like a child trying to convince the babysitter to let me eat the last chocolate bar or stay up past my bedtime.

"Yes, of course she does. But I think if she could have done things differently, she would have," Martha said, like she was stating the obvious fact that two plus two equals four.

"You know, Lisa. I know all the signs. I've lived with it more than once. You could just divorce him…"

How did this woman whom I'd held a twenty-plus-year grudge against for making me clean the refrigerator with a toothbrush understand my situation so well? How did she know what I was getting at? Was it that obvious to everyone? Why was it not obvious to me? *You don't have to listen to her,* I told myself. *Divorce is easy for her. She's been married three times, at least. What does she know about for better or for worse? Then again, she's lived it. She knows what she's talking about. And on top of it, she always comes out happy. And even her kid turned out okay. Shit.*

***

Self-diagnosis: Queen of Denial.

48 Bottles: Gambling with Our Lives
"How to bet on family."

When Jeff and I got married we were certain it would last. We felt it to our cores. With every odd against us—an out of wedlock pregnancy, a combined income of $20,000 per year, Jeff still being in school, and our ages (twenty-one and twenty-four)—we were even more determined to beat the odds. But maybe odds are odds for a reason. By early 2010, I was beginning to be tired of gambling with my life.

I wrote a true short story about a couple I knew. The man's goal was to be a professional poker player. Listening, night after night, to my girlfriend speak of this man gave me some perspective. Writing "The Gambler," I was able to draw comparisons between Robyn and Jack and Jeff and me.

The Gambler
A short story by Lisa Livingston

He was voted Apollo his senior year of high school: A God, visually anyway. Not much had changed by the time he hit his early thirties. Broad shouldered, with dark features and olive skin, he carried himself with the grace of a lion.

When she first met him, he spoke vividly of his love for poker. He bragged about how he'd racked up over ten thousand dollars at occasional weekend visits to the local casino. His brown eyes twinkled like stars when he talked of his all-time best hands—a pair of aces, trips, even the occasional full house. Jack could recall hands from four years back, when he'd started his regular ventures to the tables. There was the A-list actor, who had too much money and too much cockiness to know any better, whose money Jack was able to fleece on a regular basis. There was the old woman with the seaweed eyes who was too drunk to know any better when she went all in on a pair of sixes. And then, there was the dude in the ragged tee shirt who never knew when to quit and was more interested in the free spirits than anything else.

She listened wide-eyed, soaking up his stories and dreamt of helping him someday reach his dream of becoming a professional poker player. He'd go to the World Series and never look back. They'd sip cocktails as he asked the waiter "to get the little lady whatever she wants" and told her to order blindly from expensive menus. She'd make tiny fists under the cloth napkin on her lap, not comfortable with taking him up on his offer. At the end of the night, he pulled a wad of hundred dollar bills from his pocket, hardly looking at the check as he paid and asked her what she wanted to do next. "Anything for you, babe," he'd say with a wink.

Robyn was never one who cared much for money or the more expensive things in life. A single mother, she was comfortable with drive thru fast food joints, and the occasional fancy date out at a chain restaurant. Her favorite restaurant was Applebee's. He'd never taken her there. He wouldn't dream of it. And as time went on, she couldn't say she mind-

ed the fancier places he treated her to. Each place, each night she spent listening to his grand dreams and past winnings, were fantasies that helped her escape the simplicity of the life she'd created for herself; one she'd been quite comfortable with before him.

Plain Robyn often caught herself staring at this Apollo. What could he possibly see in me? *These insecurities led her to take special interest in learning what made Jack take a second look at her. It was, she decided, the care she took in pleasing him. There were the fish net thigh highs and stiletto heels. Short skirts and low cut sweaters. The type of girl who tripped over stones in a walkway, keeping up with Jack's preferences was not always easy for her. But she did it anyway.* Anything for Jack. He was becoming her very own God. *She knew it wasn't healthy but she didn't want to turn back.*

As time went on, Robyn realized Jack was actually a very quiet man. Unless talking about poker, he hardly opened up about other things in his life. When she pressed him, he told her he had a great family; one who supported him and had loved him hard as a child. She wasn't surprised. She hadn't expected anything less, hoping her own less-than-perfect family wouldn't be upsetting to him. As he began to trust her, Jack began to talk more about his non poker-related hopes and dreams. He spoke of a girl, Sabrina, who had broken his heart. The girl, he claimed, had thrown him out of their shared home after he began having trouble at his day job in real estate. A downward economy and poor market had left him depressed and collecting partial unemployment. Insensitive to this, Jack told Robyn that Sabrina had left him at his "weakest point". He claimed to despise her, yet Robyn knew better...

Jack's eyes lit up almost as bright as when he talked about poker when he spoke of Sabrina. For months Robyn held him as he reminisced about their five year love affair. Inside she screamed, how can this man not see that I love him more than Sabrina ever could have? *An alcoholic workaholic, Sabrina had left Jack to all the domestic chores of the home—leaving little time for him to get to the tables.* How could that bitch do such a thing? This man with such a generous heart? How could she not appreciate that? *Seeing Jack as the victim only made Robyn try harder to fully win his heart. She would do whatever she had to, at any cost.*

Her plan even worked. Years of being there for him on the sidelines eventually lead Jack to fall for Robyn in a very hard way. He took her to a restaurant one night, the fanciest he'd ever taken her to, and ordered the most expensive champagne on the menu. It was there, along the ocean, that he proposed to her over surf and turf and romantic kisses. Robyn glowed brighter than the moon for weeks as she began planning their wedding.

But the glow quickly dimmed as Robyn learned Jack hadn't exactly been truthful. After meeting his family, she learned that it was far from perfect. In fact, it made her appreciate her family—in spite of their quirks—quickly. One night brought a three-hour screaming lecture from his older brother, who insisted that Jack was a "loser". "Do you not see

273

how immature he is? He plays poker for a god dammed living." Robyn didn't know what to say, squeezing Jack's hand and defending him as much as she could, reminding his brother that Jack was the man she loved and that she'd always stand by his side. Unfortunately, Jack did not do the same. Instead, he allowed his brother to berate them both. He sat in silence. He let Robyn do the defending until she finally said it was time to go. A piece of her broke that night, realizing her Prince Charming had lied to her and hadn't had the nerve to defend her.

But love is love and she tried to put the incident out of her mind. Days later, he neglected to defend her again when Jack's father questioned, in a blunt way, "Don't you two think you are moving too fast? You don't even know each other." It was Robyn who retorted, "Actually, we've known each other for five years, hasn't Jack told you?" Again, Jack was silent, staring at his parents immaculate living room carpet and shrugging. She squeezed his hand, trying to get him to look at her. He did not.

Things like this happened over and over. Jack, living with his parents since his split with Sabrina, seemed content to follow their rules as a grown man. Robyn couldn't take much more of it. In spite of being in his mid-thirties, he worried constantly about following his controlling mother's rules.

They hadn't been engaged even two months before Jack started spending more and more time at the casino. He said he wanted to make money for them. He said he wanted to save up for them to buy a home together. He told her he needed to be with her and her two young children every day and she believed him. Knowing his great track record at the casino, Robyn encouraged him to make as much money as he could. He reminded her that poker was not a game to him, it was an occupation. And when she texted him encouraging quips like "win big tonight" or "have fun" he was instantly irritated with her.

"I'm not winning it. I'm earning it. Poker is not fun for me. Poker is a job. Don't you see how I am sacrificing for us?"

Robyn never knew what to make of his retorts, slowly training herself to replace the word 'play' with 'work' and the word 'fun' with 'safe'. But no matter how hard she tried, he became more and more irritable. She stopped encouraging him, hoping not to upset him by saying something wrong. When she asked about the sacrifices he was making, he spit back at her, "You've met my family. You think I like living with them? That place is a dungeon hell hole. I hate them all."

She'd wince, but did her best to keep Jack's spirits high. As the months went on, Jack began playing poker three or four times a week. Some weeks were good, bringing in an average of $1,000. Others were not so good, with losses of up to $800. Jack always earned more than he lost, but when totaled, his averages were about $130 a week, not counting the gas money and other funds he needed to get to the casino. Averaging about thirty hours a week at the tables, Robyn was beginning to see *that Jack's dreams of becoming a professional poker player would never support a family.*

All the while though, Jack continued to take her to expensive places, including hotel overnights, and letting her pick the best items on the menu. She found herself reminding him, again and again, that these things were unnecessary and he should be saving his money. He'd roll his eyes at her, laugh, and tell her not to worry about it. "You need to read some books on poker. You don't understand the game," he'd patronize. "You have no clue what you are talking about," he'd scold, calling her bad luck.

As they grew apart because she "ruined his concentration at work," Robyn made a conscious effort to do things Jack's way. When he announced plans to quit his $40,000 a year job to play poker fulltime, she knew better than to question him. If she questioned him, he'd say she wasn't supportive of his dreams and tell her she was just like Sabrina. He'd tell her to read a book. He'd say she didn't love him for him. She kept her mouth shut and told him to reach for his dreams and not worry about his dwindling bank account. What else can I do? The man practically hates me now. He's starting to compare me to Sabrina.

Determined to save what she could of their relationship, Robyn decided to do what she could to save the money he was trying to win at the casinos herself, through an honest day's work. She began working crazy hours. Nights, weekends, and frequent business trips out of town consumed her. If money was this important to him, she was going to

276

be sure to find a way to make it. After he said, "Sabrina was a useless bitch, but she knew how to turn a dollar into twenty," Robyn died a little bit inside. Again, his eyes were bright speaking of his ex. She was too afraid to admit what she saw in those eyes—a love for Sabrina, or at least the material things she'd provided him.

That got her to thinking. This was a grown man who had made a choice to live with parents he claimed to hate. Instead of getting his own place after Sabrina threw him out, Jack had returned to the safety of his family or origin in a home he could not smoke in, could not leave crumbs in, and where his mother still cleaned his room for him. Folded clothes, a maid for the bathroom he and his older brother shared, and a well-stocked fridge were staples of this man's life. Had Sabrina also provided these things? After all, it was her home he'd lived in, her food he'd prepared, and her that "turned a dollar into twenty".

Jack didn't look at Robyn the same way anymore. He resented the hours she worked, her medical issues, and her need to protect her children from the gypsy lifestyle he seemed to want to live; making a living as a poker player and moving on a whim to a city she did not feel was safe for them. She could see the coldness in his once warm eyes. The more time he spent at the casino, chasing his dream, the more depressed he seemed to become. Unsure of what to make of this, she tried to focus on herself— convinced her own ability to make money would diffuse his born again fantasies of Sabrina. Once interested in her work, Jack rarely asked about it anymore. After all, Robyn was supporting two children on her own and had no interest in expensive cities, restaurants, or even hotels. What Robyn craved most was stability and safety, things Jack was unwilling to try to provide all together.

As they grew even further apart, Robyn realized something: Perhaps it was not Jack who was the gambler at all. Perhaps, it was she. Now it was time to figure out exactly how to play her next hand. Everything in her told her to fold.

***

Self-diagnosis: Non-gambling wannabe.

47 Bottles: Writing It Out
"Lists: A girl's best friend."

March 19, 2010
Dear Journal,
I've got to try to write this out as objectively as possible. I know that's not going to be an easy thing to do. Sorry if I sound formal today. I need to try to keep my head about me. Emotion is what got me into this mess. I am currently at a crossroads in my life. Twice now, I have seriously considered moving out with the kids and renting an apartment on School Street. The woman who owns this particular apartment is named Becky and has been very understanding about our situation. The apartment is a two bedroom. It's on the second floor of a Victorian converted duplex. It is clean with new flooring and appliances. However, the total apartment can't be more than 900 square feet and there is no yard to speak of. On the upside, School Street would be very convenient for Nathan and Ella, who still go to school at the elementary school, only steps away. But when I brought the boys to see the apartment, they were both concerned about the stigma attached to apartment living. They said they didn't want the other kids to know that Jeff and I had separated and said they would feel "weird" and "dumb" about the whole thing if kids walked past on the way to and from school. They were worried what their peers would think. The kids never should have been exposed to any of this. A major parenting mistake on my part

that I can never take back and will always feel bad about. All I can really do is move on...

Twice now I have nixed this plan to move. I keep Becky and that little apartment in the back of my mind. Part of my reluctance to go is that I feel like Jeff should be the one to leave. While he makes more money than me and could better afford the upkeep and maintenance of the house, I am most certainly the one who will have the kids and they need consistency in their lives. I think sometimes the only thing that keeps me in my marriage is all the complications that would come from either of us moving out: Who gets the bedroom set? How do we divide the photo albums? Who gets the CDs and where do the kids' things go? Divorce is no easy matter! I guess nobody said it was.

I've made countless pros and cons lists on whether or not to end my marriage. Most people say it's always best for children to live in a stable two-parent household. However, these same people often qualify their statements with things like, "If there is no abuse or substance abuse" or "If there isn't constant fighting in the home." In my house, currently anyway, there is verbal abuse and sub-stance abuse. Our fighting has reached an almost weekly assurance for at least one blow out scream-ing session over money, alcohol, or Jeff's job.

The pros of staying are obvious. The kids would have access to both of their parents at all times in the most "normal" way possible. There would be no disruption to their living or social situations. It would help them to see how seriously we take those 'for better or worse' vows. It would teach them about loyalty, the importance of family and never quitting.

But staying could also have a bad impact on the kids. No kids are better off in a home where they know their parents are miserable together. Kids are not dumb and can sense tension. JJ, Nate, and Ella are certainly not immune to that. The more they are exposed to Jeff's alcoholism and verbal abuse, the more I worry they will grow to mimic it. Nathan worships Jeff like a god. He can do no wrong in Nate's eyes. This concerns me because what he is doing is wrong.

The plus side to leaving would be that the boys would not be around Jeff's drinking. We've agreed that if we do separate, he won't drink around the boys. That means that when they visit their father they will have his full (and sober) attention. That kind of attention from Jeff would be priceless to them and would prove to be a good role-modeling situation for them. Also, being away from Jeff and his drinking and constant mood swings would make for a much happier and more peaceful home environment all together.

But moving out also means moving on. And I'm not so sure I am ready to allow either myself or Jeff to do that completely. When Jeff is sober, he's the man I fell in love with who can make me laugh about the silliest of things. His uncanny ability to make fun of himself inspires me to be able to do the same—not bad for a girl with no self-esteem. Whether I want to admit it or not, after thirteen-plus years, I'm still in love with this man. And for that, I feel I owe him a chance. Even a hundred chances.

So here I sit, waiting at a crossroads. One eye is on the apartment, the other is firmly planted on the new living room couch set Jeff recently bought to give our growing children more space.

Pros and Cons of Staying

Pros of Staying:

* The kids need their father
*He is my best friend
*I love him
*If I leave, I have no control when he has the kids. He could drink and drive with them in the car. Or, Nathan or Ella could have an asthma attack and there'd be no way for Jeff to get them to the hospital
*Financial stability
*The kids may blame themselves if we split
*I worry about him less when he's in my line of vision, when I know what he's up to
*He may change someday
*To be able to say I stuck it out and am not a failure or a quitter
*Marriage is 'for better or worse'
*He is a good father when he's sober
*He is a good husband when he's sober
*He makes me laugh and I'd miss that
*He plays with the kids all the time and that makes them feel good
*He loves us and would be lost without us

*He's worked hard for our family and deserves to be able to have the good times with us too

*I've worked hard for our family and deserve to be able to have the good times as well

*Somehow, I still believe in him. I still believe in us

*I belong with him

*I am home when I am with him

*Ella doesn't want me to leave him

*Holidays

*Stability

Cons of Staying:

*He drinks

*He can be mean when he drinks

*His drinking will only get worse

*He could eventually get violent

*Ella doesn't want me to leave him—repeat history for her if I don't?

*The kids are witnessing this unhealthiness

*The kids may develop his habits

*Being sad

*Teaching the kids that it's okay to allow someone else to control your life

*Teaching the kids that drinking like this is okay

*Wasting my life/time and it never changes

*Being the old lady in the rocking chair. What if?

*Always wondering if I made the right decision

*I deserve more, don't I?...Do I deserve more? Do I have the right to ask for more? I mean, I did sign up for this, even if I didn't know what I was getting into...

99 Bottles

ERIN LEE

Self-diagnosis: Obsessive contemplator and planner. Plain ridiculous.

46 Bottles: They Say I Have a Right "But does that make it right?"

May 19, 2010

In the Catholic church, drunkenness for a period of seven years is grounds for an annulment. We're on year eight of this drinking crap. The funny thing? I still feel like divorcing him would be wrong. I was raised on the principle that you make your bed and you lay in it. I meant for better or for worse when I said it. So, why, even when society—including the church—tells me it's okay to get divorced, can't I shake those beliefs? And, even if I was okay with it, would I really want to leave the love of my life? No fucking way.

***

Self-diagnosis: God—or maybe religion in general—fearing. Wannabe atheist.

45 Bottles: Hating Surprises
"Writing my ending."

If you haven't figured it out by now, while I crave them, I've never been really comfortable with gray areas. Likewise, I'm not one who likes to leave things up in the air. Every year, at Christmas, when my father opens his gifts, he laughs when he gets to mine. I have a reputation of wrapping everything so tight that it takes a knife to pry the wrapping paper open. For years, he's said, "Gee. I wonder who wrapped this?" before plunging into his pocket or the coffee table drawer for his jackknife. I want my life that way; wrapped up tight and safe.

In grade school, when learning how to write a five-paragraph essay, I was probably the only child ever to write my conclusion paragraph first. While others were struggling with introductions, I was busy plotting how to wrap things up. The last thing the reader was going to see was that last paragraph, so gosh darn it had better be good.

A pathological romantic, there is nothing I enjoy more than a happy ending. I'm that annoying person who skips to the last chapter of a book to get to the ending before reading its core. I don't care if the ending is obvious. It doesn't matter if I sleep through an entire movie just to get to the ending. What I *care* about is that the protagonist is happy and everything works out. I care that the characters are satisfied, have solved their conflicts, and are working their way to happier lives. I love those predictable ending scenes in movies where the jilt-ed lovers march off together into the distance. I prefer when they do it in fancy wedding attire.

Of course, by middle age, I realized that happy endings, tidy conclusions, and even nifty Christ-mas wrap jobs aren't exactly how the real world works. It doesn't mean it irritates me any less. There is nothing more I'd love to offer readers of my story—or myself for that matter—than a happy ending. I'd even settle for any sort of conclusion at all: *Will she stay? Will she leave? How will this play out?* Your guess is as good as mine, maybe even better.

Part of me is reluctant to publish this writing un-til I find my ending. However, I promised myself that this story would be authentic. I told myself, when I began, that there would be no writing con-clusions ahead of time and no fabrication of the truth. This is my story, to date. And as much as I'd like to be able to see into the future, I've never been good with crystal balls.

What I can offer, though, is some perspective on where my life has taken me so far. I can share what I have learned about love and how I plan to use this knowledge to determine my own story's real-life ending.

***

Self-diagnosis: Seeking happy ending. (Still.)

44 Bottles: Making Sense of It
"Love is an action, not an emotion."
- Faith Chapel

When I married Farmer Charming, I thought I was signing up for "happily ever after". I believed that love was enough. I thought that if you tried your best every day, there was no way your marriage could fail. You'd simply spend your lives together, be one another's best friend, always get those crazy butterflies in your stomach when you looked at one another, and raise happy and successful children. Growing old would be more of a right than a privilege. Sure, I knew there'd be bad times, but somehow I just didn't picture 99 bottles of beer on my counter when I said, "In good times and in bad."

I've learned that love, the way most people define it, is not enough. A sign I recently passed at the trusty evangelical Faith Chapel—one of the few that ever *really* made sense to me—read, "Love is an Action, Not an Emotion." I nearly drove off the road when I read it. In fact, it changed everything.

They say there are those moments in life when you stop and everything changes. I've been looking for those moments all my life. Like a baby bird waiting for it's mother to drop the worm, I've looked to the sky and moon for signs of where to turn on my life map. But in reading the sign that day, I finally knew what they had been talking about when referring to life-changing moments. I realized something very important: If love is an action, then it's also a choice. It's very simple, really. We choose to love or not to love. We choose to continue to love or to give up that action. Confronted with such a choice, the only real decision left is to figure out which road to take.

I have loved Jeff from the moment I met him. From that day at the airport when I rubbed his back to comfort his nerves, I was loving him in an active way. I've chosen to love my Farmer Charming for fifteen years in the most beautiful moments of our marriage. I've chosen to love him for fifteen years in the most ugly moments of our marriage. I've chosen, every single day, to love him.

I haven't made this choice because I am a martyr or a victim. I have made this choice for the same selfish reason most people do—because it feels good to be loved in return. You see, Jeff's chosen to love me in both the ups and downs as well. He's sat by my hospital bed through multiple hospitalizations for chronic breathing issues. He has helped me when my depression has cropped up. He's walked away when I've done everything in my power to get him to hit me—to give me an excuse to quit our marriage. He's never cheated and he's never lied. He's been honest with me about his struggles and his imperfections. He's given me the bulk of every bonus or paycheck he has ever made. He's coached our children and rubbed my back when I couldn't sleep at night. He's encouraged and supported my obsessive love of writing. He's even been okay with me writing about our marriage and his addiction—something I think most people would be furiously anxious about.

Farmer Cowboy has built us a home—not far from New York, I might add—and makes sure we always have food in our stomachs. He's worked jobs I would never dream of working to be sure our family was okay. He's kept every promise he's ever made to me in his own way. Heck, we even have cows in our backyard! And on hot summer days, I can smell manure. A few years ago, he cleared a half acre of trees from our front yard to hang a tire swing, just for me. That is active love. He's chosen, throughout our life together, to love imperfect me. For the most part, he has made all of my childhood dreams come true.

I've also learned that love isn't perfect. People aren't perfect either. Likewise, no choice is ever perfect. Choices come with risks and loopholes. I've learned that you can't make other people's choices for them—at least not if you want them to stick. Jeff has a choice to make. He has to decide whether to keep drinking, to continue abusing his body, or to finally put the bottle down. But that decision is his and his alone. Just as I can't ask him to choose to love me, I can't ask him to choose to love himself. I trust that someday, when he is ready, he will do the right thing and that he will do it for the right reasons.

So, what *can* I do? The very best thing I can do? I can choose to love me. I can choose to love my children. And, I can continue to choose to love the man who loves me in return—for better, or for worse.

Ultimately, I may choose to walk away. But that's a choice Jeff could make at any time too. By no means do I claim that I am easy to live with. (It's got to be hard living with someone so big on control, lists, and happy endings.) I've always taken for granted that he will continue to love me, forever, because that's what Farmer Charming does. But I know now that you can't count on fairy tales, happy endings, or even forever. What you can count on is yourself and faith in something bigger than you; God, a higher power, spirituality, or this blessed thing we call life. I believe there is something bigger than the sum of us. And, for as long as I can have faith in that thing, I can have faith in myself that I'll make the right choices—for me, and for the people I choose to love.

***

Self-diagnosis: Becoming self-defined. Okay being me, for now. And that's enough.

43 Bottles: Butterfly Girl
"Just when the caterpillar thought
it was over, she became a butterfly."
– Anonymous

That's where my story ended, half a decade ago. It hasn't been until now that I could pick up the pen. The events that happened since 2010 have been just too tough to write about. With the help of a new therapist and Mr. J, I'm finally ready to finish this part of our story.

It was late 2012 by the time I had the courage to give Jeff an ultimatum. By then, Ella was becoming interested in boys and I could see the way she viewed her father as a hero. Watching an entirely sober Jeff and Ella go off to a father-daughter's dance at the recreation department made me see things from a whole different perspective. It was then that I saw her as a future wife, partner, and mother. All I could think about was the kind of man she might choose: *Would she, like me, think that there were good drunks out there? Would she clean up after her husband's messes, hiding empty bottles from friends and family? Would she ever be big enough to help carry a grown man to bed?* Ella, a free spirit and budding artist by then, still had the adoring eyes of an innocent child but those eyes were beginning to wander. It wasn't something I could ignore. Sure, most of Jeff's drinking went on well after she was tucked away for the night. But I wasn't naive enough to think she didn't know what was going on. We spoke about it too freely. His beers, nine at a time every other night, still lined the counter tops and our sons didn't hesitate to joke about them. What they were old enough to understand was a real problem for their father, she viewed as normal. I was not okay with that.

I asked Jeff to get help that fall. I wanted him to do a thirty-day in-patient program at Phoenix House, a treatment facility in a nearby town. I made it my mission for a month to research payment options and to push portions of it through my company's insurance plan. And, after a brutal fight that led to me calling the police and him being escorted to a cheap motel, he finally agreed. He wasn't in the program more than a week before he'd checked himself out and called me, crying, begging to come home. I, of course, let him. *Ella misses him. It wasn't so bad,* I lied to myself.

Two more failed attempts at recovery and my own ability to finally say "no," and the fourth time was the charm. Jeff earned his first thirty-day Alcoholics Anonymous chip in January of 2015. He wouldn't let me attend the meeting where he spoke about his journey and didn't say much about it either. He let Ella hold his chip, but wouldn't look me in the eye. I figured it wouldn't last and was just about to give up, for good. But thirty days turned to ninety and ninety to one hundred and twenty. By September,

Ella's birthday, I began to believe everything might really be okay. As we sent JJ off to college in North Carolina, Jeff and I made attempts to rediscover each other. With Nathan driving and Ella becoming more independent, we started off slowly with date nights. Date nights grew into weekend get-a-ways; the first in our marriage that didn't involve a buzz or the possibility of a hangover for Jeff.

It wasn't perfect. There were many fights and I knew better than to get my hopes up. He slipped three times but always followed up with AA meetings and calling his sponsor. I became a regular at meetings for enablers; knowing I was as much a part of the problem as he was. I fought off urges to offer him beer every time he came home stressed. I resented not being able to drink myself, missing JJ and wishing I could soften that loss with a sip of wine. But it was close enough. I was proud of us for admitting our weaknesses and doing everything we could to patch together a new relationship. It felt amazing to have my Farmer Charming back, scars and all. Life was looking exactly how I'd planned it so many years before.

**

Dec. 10, 2015

I can't believe this day is finally here. I haven't seen JJ since dropping him off in Greensboro for preseason soccer practices at college.

I'm excited to have him home with us for a month for the holidays; to show him that things really *have* changed. I'm anxious to begin our fourteen-hour ride to pick him up and bring him home. I've never liked long car rides. I get too fidgety. But Jeff has promised Nathan and Ella we can stop at Arby's.

Nathan rolls his eyes at me when I insist we sing songs to make the ride go faster. He puts on his wireless headphones and watches videos on his phone. Ella humors me, singing Christmas carols and playing the alphabet game with Jeff and I. Jeff wins. Nathan takes off his headphones when it's time to play trivia, a game Jeff invented when the kids were young. Nathan's good at trivia and picks the category of cars. Ella complains, saying she wishes she had a sister. She tells Jeff she will someday marry a farmer and live in Maryland. They won't play this "dumb game" in the car. They won't sing either. Somehow, I'm sad for her.

An hour out of New Jersey, I begin to fall asleep. I eavesdrop on Ella, who's never been able to sleep in cars, and Jeff, who enjoys company on long drives. They talk about Ella's plans to become a veterinarian. Someday, she says, she will have chickens and a rooster. The rooster will be her alarm clock. She will take care of large-breed animals and have only one kid—a daughter named Lotus—who will help her. Lotus, she explains is the name of both a flower and a car. Jeff laughs, telling her she has her whole life planned out. He reminds her that things can change and not to get too worried about a plan just yet.

"What if your husband wants to name her Corvette?" Jeff teases.

"Oh, Dad. Whatever. Shut up. A girl has to do everything. If we have to be the pregnant ones, we get the final say on the name. My husband's going to know that. He's not going to be like a jerk, you know. Geesh."

"Well that's good! I can't see me letting a jerk past the front porch," he jokes, sort of. I, who has been privy to his late night ramblings about who will and who will not be allowed to pick our daughter up for dates, try not to laugh. I remember the day Ella and I shopped for her first non-training bra. "Black? Really, Lisa? Are you trying to send me to the grave?" he'd asked. I'd told him to chill out and told him that black was just what happened to be on sale.

Ella snaps her gum. "You can't just, like, pick for me, Dad. I get to pick for myself and I know exactly what I'm going to pick. He's going to be…"

Tires squeal. My neck thrusts forward and my body moves so fast toward the dashboard that I can't lift my head to see what's happening. Jeff curses. Our car slides off the side of the highway, over the breakdown lane, into…something. I grip the passenger handle. Ella screams. A noise, louder than any explosion—like a bomb—cuts a quick second of silence before it's sudden return. I'm pushed tight against my seatbelt and an airbag slams my face, breaking my nose and sending pain through me like I've never known. And more silence.

**

I don't remember much more than that. I can't think about it for long; the accident that took my Farmer Charming from me. What I remember most is emptiness. I felt it for months. Even with my three children by my side, I could feel nothing but the hole not having Jeff with us had burnt into me; into us.

JJ flew home, giving up his soccer scholarship. I'm not sure what I would have done without him. He took a semester off and will transfer to the local community college eventually. He says he can't leave us yet. Honestly, I'm not ready to let him go. Our broken bones—my nose, jaw, collarbone; Ella's femur and knee; Nathan's arms and left wrist. They've all healed. We're left with scars and memories.

I close my eyes, trying not to look at her. I sit in the third row of the courthouse, waiting for the man who hit us to be arraigned. A woman, with a butterfly scarf, sits in another aisle, second row. I watch her as she uses her scarf to mop her eyes. I know she must be his wife. She's alone, she's afraid. She probably enables him. She is no different than I was, only a year ago. I wonder how many children they've had and what name she calls him—this man who killed my husband, shattered our dreams. I sense that she wants to look at me. I've felt her

297

gaze but refuse to make eye contact. I'm not ready. I want to scream at her. I want to ask her why she didn't get him into treatment, why she let him drive. I want to know why she didn't know about good drunks verses bad ones. Responsible verses the kind she'd obviously married; who kills families and steals dreams.

I squeeze Nathan's hands. They are shaking. The judge walks in, and Nathan rises. I know we're supposed to stand, but it takes everything in me to just lean up against the back of the seat in front of us, to half-stand, before sitting back down. Nathan takes longer to sit. I know he wants to jump over the bench, to get to the man who killed his father. I know he wants to hit him. He's just like his father. I tug softly at his sweater, reminding him he has to follow the rules. We will get justice, somehow, this gesture reminds him. Or, I hope it does. And I hope we will. I think.

Ella leans on JJ. He rubs her hair. She glares at the back of the man's head as he's escorted in, cuffed, shackled, and wearing an orange too bright for my tear-stained eyes. I look away. She doesn't. She mouths, "I hate you." JJ tells her to be quiet. He says, "Stay cool, El." She presses her face into his chest and he tightens his grip on her shoulder.

I look back to the woman. It occurs to me she's like Jeff's mistress, Mrs. Lebatt's: The one I hated so much for all those years. I'd invited her into my home. I'd let her stay and even encouraged his love for her. I'd used her to help placate him in fights or times of stress. The woman, whose name I've only read in papers, shifts, trying to get a better view of her husband. He doesn't look back at her. She strains her neck, coughs, and finally settles back in her seat. I wonder what she's thinking. I want revenge, but don't know how to need it. What I *need*, is to forgive.

***

My name is Lisa.
I'm forty-two years old.
Somewhere along the way, I stopped diagnosing myself.
Why?
Because:
This is my story.

I'm a single mother of three.
I'm a daughter.
I'm a sister.
I am an enabler and the widow of an alcoholic.
I'm more than a number on a scale.
I'm more than any diagnosis, self-inflicted or not.
I'm a dreamer who deserves to realize her wishes.
I'm better than the men and boys I've thrown myself so desperately at in hopes of finding love.

I am responsible for no one's actions but my own.

I'm not alone.
I'm not scared.
I'm empowered.
I'm alive.
I'm human.
I still wear his ring.

And, in finally putting it all out there, I'm also brave.

Acknowledgements

Special thanks to Taylor Henderson, who edited this book for me. Taylor has become one of my closest friends in the indie author community. I don't know what I'd do without her kind-natured friendship and bits of spunk that keep me laughing through the process. Nights of "D" games and passive aggressive #nothanks keep me going.

Thank you, too, to Ebony McMillian, my PA, who always has my back; even when it's just converting a time zone. Ebony is a kindred spirit. I cannot imagine how I survived writing full novels pre Ebony. Thank you!

Thank you to Dbear who lived through the 'J experience' with me and helped me work through it.

I'd also like to thank the people who have had the courage to share their experiences with me. Your honesty has been eye-opening and renewed my faith in the human spirit. In my book, no matter what you've decided, you're all butterflies. I mean it when I say, "This is *our* story."

Thank you to the alcoholics I've known and loved. It used to be pretty easy to pass judgement on you. I couldn't understand why anyone would continue such destructive behaviors when they had a 'choice' to quit. Because of you, I've been able to look back at my own life and places where I've made similar mistakes and didn't know how to change. I now understand the disease that you struggle with. I wish you peace and pray you find the answers you need to get there.

Thank you to the person who called me out on keeping secrets. You were right, I don't believe in secrets and should never have kept my own. One of the best things about life is that you continue to grow. My growth is something I'm proud of and you played a huge role in that: Thank you!

I could not have written this book without taking a class on alcoholism and substance abuse during my graduate school training for family therapy. Special thanks to my professor, Dr. Walter Lowe, who taught me a new, compassionate way to look at alcoholics and the people who love them: "It's a lot easier to point fingers and call names than to dig deeper." Yes, Walter, it is. But, once you *do* dig deeper, it's also easier to look in the mirror too. Thank you for forcing me to face my own demons.

A special thanks goes out to my readers, who have been aware of this project for years and have checked in to see how it was going. I know it's been a long wait. I apologize. I hope, that in finally reading it, you understand why. Your encouragement to release *99 Bottles* is exactly what made it happen. I could not do this without you.

Finally, my deepest thanks goes to the one person who taught me that love is a verb, not a noun. And—*boy, oh boy*—what a verb it has been: To believe, hope, trust, hurt, feel, hate, resent, forgive, and back again. My heart is forever yours, no matter where our lives take us. 'They' tell us writers to write about what scares us. For years, I told 'them' to piss off. I just wasn't ready. You have encouraged me to do that at all costs. Your bravery to admit your own flaws and ability to overlook

302

mine are things I will forever be in awe of. *Your* courage inspired me to finish this project, so long in the making. With this, *we* are free. (Enjoy the Skyline on me). I love you, ***actively***, no matter how near and no matter how far.

99 Bottles

Book Club Discussion Questions

1. Why do men and women stay with alcoholics who refuse treatment, knowing what their lives will likely look like?

2. Would Lisa have married Jeff if she had a crystal ball and could see into their future together? What are her regrets? What's her biggest achievement?

3. What role does Lisa play in her husband's ongoing struggle with alcoholism? Did she contribute to his drinking by enabling it? Or, is the blame strictly on him?

4. What impact will Jeff's drinking all those years have on Ella's choices around the life partner she one-day picks?

5. Who, if any, are the victims in this story? Is Lisa a victim of, or participant in, Jeff's drinking?

6. Who, if any, are the villains?

7. What motivated Lisa to stay in her marriage? What motivated Jeff?

8. What impact did living in this situation for the majority of their childhoods have on Jeff and Lisa's children?

9. What are your personal experiences with alcoholics and addicts? Can they ever fully recover and change?

10. Will Jeff and Lisa's children become alcoholic, growing up in a home like this? Why or why not?

11.   How do you view alcoholism—as a choice, a disease, or both? Why?

12.   How many people do you know—self included—who struggle with drinking or other substance abuse? What impact has it had on your relationships?

13.   What role did Lisa and Jeff's own families of origins play in shaping who they became as adults?

14.   Was Lisa strong or weak and when?

15.   What will Lisa and her children do now?

16.   Why, when Jeff and Lisa were finally able to change, was Jeff killed? What role did alcohol play in their lives? Was it the cement that glued them, or did it tear them apart? Had Jeff lived, would they have been able to remain in a sober relationship together long term? Why or why not?

17.   What lessons does *99 Bottles* teach about alcoholics and the people who love them?

For more Information on Alcohol-ism:

Adult Children of Alcoholics Worldwide Service
Organization
www.adultchildren.org
P.O.Box 3216
Torrance CA 90510
310-534-1815

Al-anon/Alateen
www.al-anon.org
1600 Corporate Landing Parkway
Virginia Beach, VA 23454

Alcohol and Drug Problems Association of
North America
www.adpana.com
307 North Main
St. Charles MO, 63301
314-589-6702

Alcohol Beverage Medical Research Foundation
1122 Kenilworth Drive, Suite 407
Baltimore, MD 21204
410-821-7066

Alcohol Policy Network
www.apolnet.ca
Ontario Public Health Association
700 Lawrence Avenue West, Suite 310
Toronto, Ontario

99 Bottles
Canada, M6A 3B4
416-367-3313

Alcoholics Anonymous
www.aa.org
P.O. Box 459
Pennsylvania, NY 10163
212-870-3400

American Council on Alcoholism
www.aca-usa.org
1000 E Indian School Rd.
Phoenix, AZ 85014
800-527-5344
info@aca-usa.org

American Foundation for Addiction Research
www.addictionresearch.com
P.O. Box 2112
Carefree, AZ 85377
480-368-2688

Co-Dependents Anonymous
www.coda.org
PO Box 33577
Phoenix, A.Z. 85067 (602) 277.7991

Drug Abuse Resistance Education (DARE)
www.dare.com
9800 La Cienega Blvd., Suite 401
Inglewood, CA 90301

Mother's Against Drunk Driving
www.madd.org
511 E. John Carpenter Freeway. Suite 700
Irving, TX 75062
800-GET-MADD (438-6233)

National Association of Addiction Treatment
Providers (NAATP)
www.naatp.org
313 W. Liberty Street, Suite 129
Lancaster, PA 17603-2748
717-392-8480

National Council on Alcoholism and Drug De-
pendence (NCADD)
www.ncadd.org
12 West 21st Street
Pennsylvania, NY 10010
800-622-2255

National Institute on Alcohol Abuse and Alcoholism
National Institutes of Health
www.niaaa.nih.gov
5635 Fishers Lane, MSC 9304
Bethesda, MD 20892-9304
301-443-3860

National Organization for Fetal Alcohol Syn-
drome
www.nofas.org
900 17th Street, NW, Suite 910

Washington, DC 20006
202-785-4585

Partnership for a Drug-Free America
www.drugfree.org
405 Lexington Avenue, Suite 1601
Pennsylvania, NY 10174
212-966-1560

Substance Abuse and Mental Health Services
Administration
ncadi.samhsa.gov
P.O. Box 2345
Rockville, MD 20847
800-729-6686

Women for Sobriety
www.womenforsobriety.org
P.O. Box 618
Quakertown, PA 18951
(215) 536-8026

About the Author

Erin Lee is a freelance writer and therapist living with her family in southern New Hampshire. She is the author of *Crazy Like Me*, a novel published in 2015 by Savant Books and Publications, LLC. She is also author of *Wave to Papa*, 2015, *Nine Lives*, 2016, and *Alters*, 2016 with Limitless Publishing. She also penned *Host, Merge, Her Name Was Sam* and *When I'm Dead*. She is the author of *Losing Faith* with Black Rose Writing. In her free time, she works on her upcoming releases, *Just Things, From Russia, With Love, Take Me As I Am, The Morning After,* and *(The Trouble With) Butterfly Kisses*.

Lee holds a master's degree in psychology and works with at-risk families and as a court appointed special advocate. She also has special training in substance abuse and alcoholism.

***

Let's Connect!

Erin Lee's work can be found at:
www.authorerinlee.com,
on Goodreads, Author Erin Lee,
on Facebook at:
www.facebook.com/gonecrazytalksoon
and on twitter at @Crazylikeme2015.

***

This is a work of fiction. Names, characters, places, and incidents are either the product of the author's imagination or are used fictitiously and/or have been altered to suit the story. This book is not a memoir, though many of the author's life experiences with alcoholism and alcohol have been written about here in memoir form. **Repeat: This book is *not* a memoir. It is a work of literary fiction based on collective events and stories, including those of this author: Think Sylvia Plath's *Bell Jar.***

***

CRAZY
INK

ISBN-13: 978-1519306128
ISBN-10: 1519306121

www.ingramcontent.com/pod-product-compliance
Lightning Source LLC
Chambersburg PA
CBHW061957280526
45787CB00005B/1899